P9-DNN-865

Meals for Good Health

By Karen M. Graham

Registered Dietitian (R.D.)

Certified Diabetes Educator (C.D.E.)

Published in co-operation with the

To my many clients over the years who were my inspiration to write this book.

PAPER BIRCH PUBLISHING
89 Wilkinson Crescent
Portage la Prairie, Manitoba R1N 1A7 Canada

Canadian Cataloguing in Publication Data

Graham, Karen, 1959-
Meals for Good Health
Published in co-operation with the
Canadian Diabetes Association.
Includes index.
ISBN 1-55056-569-9
1. Diabetes--Diet therapy--Recipes. 2. Heart--Diseases--Diet therapy--Recipes. 3. Low-fat diet--Recipes. 4. Menus--Planning.
I. Canadian Diabetes Association. II. Title.
RC662.G73 1998 641.5631 C98-920037-X

This book was financially supported in part by the National Literacy Secretariat, Human Resources Development Canada.

EDITORIAL ASSISTANT: JANICE MADILL
PHOTOGRAPHY: BRIAN GOULD PHOTOGRAPHY INC.
FOOD STYLIST: JUDY FOWLER
BOOK DESIGN: STEVE PENNER
PRINTED AND BOUND IN CANADA BY: FRIESENS CORPORATION

Cover photo: Pita Sandwich (page 87)

Words of Thanks

A vision for this book was shared with the National Literacy Secretariat, Manitoba Education and Training (Adult Literacy and Continuing Education Branch), the Portage la Prairie Lions Club and the Canadian Diabetes Association. I thank them for the encouragement and support they gave to me.

I am very grateful to my plain language editors, who helped make this book easy-to-read and made sure it had just the right amount of information for you. Thank you to Janice Madill and Joanne Godin.

My thanks to the dietitians who reviewed my book: Dr. Diane Morris, Cynthia Abbott Hommel, Nina Kudriakowski; and to Kristin Anderson and Wendy Graham of the Canadian Diabetes Association's 1996 National Nutrition Committee. Thank you to Kathy Younker who assisted with the nutrient analysis and the final nutritional review.

Thanks to those who helped with reviews and evaluations: Douglas Graham, Wilma Koersen, Helena Haberman, Theresa Harper, Kathyrn Hockley, Maureen Kitson, Shelly Lovett, Anna Ling, France Marcoux and Andrea Tschikota. A thank you to Carol Pshebnicki who helped me develop many of the recipes. My thanks also to those who shared recipe ideas, including Madeline Coopsammy, Ellen and Dieter Mulitze, Mildred Narvey and Bill Protopapas. Thank you to those who helped in other ways, especially, Murray Graham, Linda Omichinski and Margaret and Leo Durand.

It is true that a picture is worth a thousand words. Thank you to Brian Gould and Judy Fowler for the beautiful photographs.

A very special thanks to my parents, Marg and Bill Graham, for their many reviews and their wonderful encouragement.

To Rick Durand, my lifelong companion, and our children, Carl and Roslyn, thank you for making this adventure fun and complete.

Contents

Getting Started

Do you want to lose weight, but you don't want to go on a diet? Do you have diabetes, high cholesterol or high blood pressure and want to know what you should eat? Do you want to know how to look and feel healthy? These are important questions. My name is Karen Graham and I am a Registered Dietitian. I have talked to over three thousand people in fifteen years of nutrition counseling. Most of my clients have diabetes or heart disease. Many are overweight. They range in age from children to seniors. I answer these questions for all my clients, and I do not put them on a diet.

If you were a new client, I would ask you what you had eaten over the past few days. I would then work out how many calories you had eaten. You might be surprised to find out that you eat a lot of calories each day. Many calories are hidden in the foods we eat.

Once we know how many calories you eat in a day, I could show you how to start eating less. I would put two plates on the table. On the first plate I would place actual-size plastic food models to show you how much you eat at your usual meal. On the second plate I would place food models for the same meal, but I would remove some meat and some butter or margarine and put on more vegetables. The second plate would have the food you like to eat but in different portions and with fewer calories.

You can eat the foods you love and still lose weight.

My actual-size food models would show you exactly how much food you should eat to lose weight. However, once you got home it would be hard for you to remember the portions I showed you in my office. This is how I thought of the idea for *Meals for Good Health*—a book you can take home that has actual-size photographs of healthy meals, and recipes.

With *Meals for Good Health*, you don't need to worry about counting calories or weighing and measuring your food portions. You only have to look at the actual-size photographs.

The nutrition information in this book is based on the recommendations of *Canada's Food Guide to Healthy Eating* and the Canadian Diabetes Association's *Pocket Food Guide.*

These recommendations include:

- choose a variety of foods every day
- choose foods in moderation
- eat regular meals
- eat less fat
- eat more starchy foods and fruits and vegetables
- eat more high-fiber foods
- enjoy eating well, being active and feeling good about yourself

***Meals for Good Health* is in two parts.**

Part 1—*Ideas for Healthy Living*

The first part of the book will give you tips for losing weight slowly and will tell you how to keep the weight off. There are ideas on how to eat less food, how to eat less fat and how to start exercising more. You will learn about healthy eating. You will find advice about diabetes and heart disease.

The first part of ***Meals for Good Health*** *has ideas for healthy eating and losing weight.*

Part 2—*Meals, Recipes and Snacks*

I have learned that people need more than recipes to plan their meals. *Meals for Good Health* will show you meals, recipes and snacks for each day of the month. For each meal there are two photographs. The actual-size photograph shows a large meal and the second photograph shows a smaller meal. **You will be able to see exactly how much food to eat.** The pictures are so real-looking you may want to eat them right off the pages!

The second part has meals and recipes.

It is difficult to lose weight, and I understand that well. If you use the tips, recipes, meals and snacks that I have included in *Meals for Good Health*, you will lose weight slowly. You will feel better once you are eating healthy foods and exercising. If you lose one or two pounds a month, you will be doing great.

So, let's get started.

Sweetened with Aspartame
Cholesterol Free
ONLY 10 CALORIES PER 1/2 CUP
PINK SALMON

Ideas for Healthy Living

Making Changes

As you get older, you need less to eat.

Changing how you eat will take time. The biggest change will be eating less food. It is true that we get fat because we eat too much food and we don't exercise enough.

During my counseling sessions, some people tell me they don't eat a lot of food. But if you eat the same amount of food as you did when you were ten years younger, and you have gained weight, then you are eating too much food. As you get older you need less food because your body slows down and you are not as active.

When you eat more food than your body needs, the extra food is changed into body fat. It does not matter whether that extra food is meat, cookies or butter; the extra food becomes body fat.

Here are some tips to help you lose weight and gain health.

Drink water

I counsel everyone to drink water. Water is good for you and it has no calories. It helps to fill your stomach. Drinking water is so important for losing weight that I have written a whole chapter about water.

Fill up on vegetables and fruit

These foods are naturally low in fat and are full of fiber, vitamins and minerals. If you eat more vegetables and fruit, you will find it easier to cut back on meats, fats, desserts and high-fat snack foods.

Eat breakfast

Do you eat breakfast? Many of the people I counsel do not. They say they are not hungry in the morning and they do not want the extra calories. They are not hungry in the morning because they eat too big a dinner and lots of evening snacks. In the morning, they are still full from the night before.

When you eat breakfast, even a piece of fruit or a slice of toast, you have more energy. Your body will also "switch on" and start using up your fat. If you overeat in the evening, when you are less active, your body will store fat.

Let me suggest two changes. First, start eating a small breakfast. Second, eat less in the evening.

Use a smaller plate

Here's a little trick: Use a smaller plate, and your smaller portions will still look like a lot of food.

Eat slowly

We have all eaten too quickly, then later said "I'm stuffed." Slow down and enjoy a smaller amount of food, for a little longer.

Save leftovers for the next meal

My grandmother used to say she got fat on shame because "it was a shame to see food go to waste."

Brush your teeth

Brush your teeth after a meal or snack. This may help keep you from feeling hungry so soon. I find this is a good way to stop overeating in the evening.

Go grocery shopping only after you've eaten

If I am hungry when I go grocery shopping, I am easily tempted to buy cakes and extra snacks. I try to go shopping after a meal. Then I can control myself and stay away from high-fat snacks and desserts. It works, try it.

Limit restaurant meals

I suggest that you limit restaurant meals. Restaurant meals may seem to be a treat, but they are often high in fat and sugar. In a month of meals *Meals for Good Health* shows you just a few restaurant meals. These meals could also be made at home.

Weigh yourself no more than once a month

Your body weight goes up and down every day by one or two pounds, so it's not a good idea to weigh yourself every day. If you weigh yourself once a month, you will notice a gradual weight loss. If you lose one or two pounds a month you are doing well, because these pounds will stay off.

If you do not have a weigh scale, have your doctor or dietitian weigh you at least once a year.

If you are overweight by forty or fifty pounds, it probably took ten or more years to put that weight on. Expect to lose weight slowly. Losing ten pounds in one year would be a great success for anyone.

Go for a walk

Walking makes you feel better and helps you lose weight.

Try making these small changes. These changes are a great way to start losing weight. Read on and you'll learn about some other changes that you can make when you are ready.

Eating Less Fat

An important way to reduce calories and lose weight is to eat less fat. Eating less fat is also better for your heart and can lower your risk for some kinds of cancer.

What is fat? There are two kinds of fat: vegetable fat and animal fat. Many people tell me they use 100 percent vegetable margarine and oil, with no cholesterol. I agree these are good choices. But vegetable fats still have the same number of calories as butter or lard, which are animal fats. Fat is fattening, whether it's vegetable fat or animal fat. We need to eat less of all kinds of fat.

Margarine has about the same calories as butter.

Vegetable fats include margarine, shortening and all vegetable oils, such as corn oil, canola oil and olive oil. Vegetable fats are found in salad dressings and mayonnaise. They are added to many foods, such as potato chips, crackers and muffins.

Animal fats and cholesterol are found in meats such as beef, pork, chicken and fish, and processed meats such as bacon and bologna. They are also found in eggs, cheese, whole milk, cream, lard, butter and gravy.

Many people believe bread and potatoes are fattening, so they cut down on these foods. But in fact what is fattening is the fats that we add to the bread and potatoes. Eating too much butter, margarine and gravy is what makes you put on weight. Use less of these.

A teaspoon of fat has twice as many calories as a teaspoon of starch.

Let's go on a grocery tour and look for hidden fat!

I take my clients on tours of grocery stores. Here are some of the things we talk about.

- Food labels list the amount of fat. Fat is listed in grams. Five grams (5 g) of fat is the same as 1 teaspoon of fat. On a box of crackers, serving sizes will vary. If one serving of three to five crackers has 5 g of fat, you will eat a whole teaspoon of fat when you eat those three crackers. That is a lot of hidden fat. A serving of three to five crackers with 2 g of fat or less would be a good choice.

- Foods labeled as *light* or *lite* may have less fat in them than the regular brands. Compare the labels of the light brand with the regular brand. Buy the one with the least amount of fat. For example, *light* hot chocolate has less fat and less sugar than regular hot chocolate. When a food is labeled as *light*, however, it may simply mean that the food is a light color. So check the label before you buy a food.

- *Low-fat* foods are usually good choices. These foods have less vegetable fat and less animal fat than the regular brands. One serving of a low-fat food must have less than about half a teaspoon of fat. Look for low-fat mayonnaise, low-fat margarine and low-fat cheese.

- *Calorie-reduced* foods are also good choices. They have fewer calories because they have less fat or sugar than the regular brand.

- One tablespoon of *fat-free* or *oil-free* salad dressing or *fat-free* sour cream has very little fat and very few calories. These are good choices.

- When a label says *cholesterol-free* the food will be low in cholesterol and animal fat (saturated fat) but it may still be loaded with vegetable fat and calories. For example, frozen french fries labeled *cholesterol-free* are made with vegetable oil. Remember, animal fat and vegetable fat have the same high number of calories.

Check the label and choose foods that are:
- *light*
- *low-fat*
- *calorie-reduced*
- *fat-free*

A food that has fewer than 10 calories in a serving is so low in calories that it will not have an effect on your weight.

- On the tour we look at the amount of fat in milk, and we talk about what kinds of milk are best for most adults. In whole milk, half the calories come from fat. This is not a good choice, as we do not need all this fat. By choosing 2 percent milk, you will get less fat than in whole milk. In 1 percent milk, one-quarter of the calories still come from fat, but this is a better choice than 2 percent milk. Skim milk is fat-free so is the best choice for most adults. It may take time to get used to the new taste of skim milk, but it is a refreshing drink.

Note: *On a label, % M.F. (percent milk fat) or % B.F. (percent butter fat) tells you how much fat is in a food, such as milk or cheese. Choose the one with the lowest percent fat.*

- We also look carefully at the luncheon meats, such as salami and bologna, and sausages and bacon. These meats have a lot of fat. Try to buy fewer of these and choose instead lean slices of ham, chicken, turkey or roast beef. A couple of the meals in this book do include a high-fat meat choice, such as wieners or sausages, but you'll see that because of the fat, the portions are small.

- Last on the tour, we check the amount of fat and sugar in cookies, cakes and snacks. There are many low-fat crackers, such as soda crackers, melba toast and rice cakes. You may also be able to find baked snack foods with no added fat, for example, baked corn chips. These are good choices.

  All cookies and cakes have some fat and sugar. Arrowroot biscuits, social teas and angel food cake are not as rich in fat as others.

  Some cookies or chocolate bars may be marked as *carbohydrate-reduced* or *sugar-free*. These may contain other sweeteners, such as sorbitol, and they may have a lot of fat added to them.

I *suggest that my clients try to avoid the bakeshop and the chip and cookie aisles when they go shopping.*

- Sometimes a label will not show how much fat or sugar is in the food. You will see only the ingredients listed. It is important to know that the first ingredients listed are the main ingredients. For example, if vegetable or palm oil is listed first, you will know the food is high in fat. If sugar, honey or glucose is listed first, this means the food is high in sugar.

More tips to help you eat less fat.

Add less fat to your food

Before you put butter, margarine, mayonnaise, cream or gravy on your food, ask yourself if you really need it. Try eating less of these fats. When you want a topping or spread, try a small amount of one of the low-fat or fat-free brands.

Take the fat off meat, chicken and fish

Trim the fat off meats, and take the skin off chicken, turkey or fish before cooking. Chicken or fish with the skin left on can have just as much fat as fatty red meats.

Cook foods without adding fat

Many foods can be cooked in fat-free ways. Foods can be boiled, steamed, broiled or barbecued. Try steamed fish, broiled sausages or chicken, or barbecued corn on the cob. If you occasionally want to fry foods, use a non-stick pan and don't add fat. Or cook in a heavy pan with some water or broth, or use a cooking spray, so the food doesn't stick to the pan.

Low-fat baking tip:

Cut out at least half the fat called for in cake and muffin recipes. To keep your muffins or cake moist, add a small amount of skim milk yogurt or applesauce, as in the muffin recipe on page 64.

Eat less meat, chicken and fish

Now that you have cut off the extra fat and you are cooking without fat, you should try eating less of the meat, chicken and fish. Even if they are lean, they will still have some hidden fat.

Try other flavorings on vegetables

Lightly cook your vegetables and they will be more tasty. Then sprinkle them with lemon juice or spices instead of butter or margarine. A sprinkle of dill, parsley, pepper or garlic can really make your vegetables taste good.

Put less fat on your sandwiches

Spread your sandwiches with a small amount of salsa, mustard, relish or light mayonnaise. Limit added fat.

Congratulations! You are now eating much less fat.

Drinking More Water

Dietitians suggest drinking eight glasses of water a day. Eight glasses equals a two-liter plastic soft drink bottle. Many of us get much of our water in our coffee, tea, juice or soft drinks each day. But our bodies don't need all the caffeine or sugar in these drinks. Feel free to drink some coffee, tea or diet soft drinks, but also drink lots of plain water. It is the best calorie-free food.

Drink 8 glasses of water each day.

It is a good habit to regularly drink water. Water helps keep you regular. Water helps reduce your thirst when you exercise.

Here are some tips to help you start drinking more water.

Remind yourself

Often we simply forget to drink water. If you like water cold, keep a bottle or jug of water in the fridge. Keep a water glass on your table. When you see the jug or glass, you will remember to drink water.

Drink water in the morning

We are naturally thirsty when we first wake up. Drink water first thing in the morning.

Drink water with meals

Get into the habit of having one glass of water or more with all your meals and snacks. Add a slice of lemon to your water for a fresh taste.

Drink water whenever you feel hungry

Water fills your stomach so you feel full and eat less.

Water makes life flow. Go with the flow.

Eating More Starches

Grains and other starches:
- *give you energy*
- *are low in fat*
- *help you feel full*
- *have fiber*

Have a starch food with every meal.

Grains and starches are the staple foods for most people around the world. They include grains, such as wheat and oats, corn, rice, potatoes, lentils, beans and cassava. Grains and starches are made into breakfast cereals and are ground into flour to make breads, pitas, tortillas, noodles, bannocks and rotis.

Starches provide energy, are low in fat and are low in cost. They are bulk foods that help us feel full. Starches add vitamins and minerals to our diet.

Fiber is another important part of many starch foods, such as whole wheat or rye breads. Fiber is a natural laxative. Much of the fiber has been taken out of white flour.

The North American diet has changed over the last century. We now eat fewer starch foods and we eat more meat and processed foods. Processed foods have fat, sugar and salt added. So we are eating more fat. We suffer from diseases that are linked to eating too much fat, such as diabetes, heart disease and cancer.

Losing weight means eating less fat. That usually means eating less meat and less added fat. Starch and vegetables will start filling up more of your plate.

You will find that all the meals in *Meals for Good Health* include grains or starches, with little or no added fat.

Grains and Starches

Filling Up on Vegetables & Fruits

Vegetables and fruits are low in fat.

Eating vegetables and fruits gives you energy. They are low in fat. Like starch foods, they add vitamins, minerals and extra fiber to your diet.

Fresh or frozen vegetables and fruits are the best. Check the label and choose frozen ones that do not have salt, fat or sugar added.

Fruit canned in water or juice is a better choice than fruit canned in syrup. Drain off most of the juice. Canned vegetables usually have salt, and sometimes sugar, added. Choose these less often.

Fresh fruit is better than juice. Drink water, not juice, if you are thirsty.

You may be surprised to learn that "unsweetened" fruit juices have sugar. One cup of unsweetened apple, orange or grapefruit juice has 6 to 7 teaspoons of natural sugar. Grape and prune juice have almost 10 teaspoons of sugar in a cup. Since juice has less fiber and is not as filling as fresh fruit, it is easy to drink too much. If you drink a lot of juice, it will be hard for you to lose weight.

Vegetable juices, such as tomato juice, have less sugar than fruit juices. For this reason, several meals in *Meals for Good Health* include a small glassful. When you are thirsty, drink water, not juices.

Dried fruit has more sugar than fresh fruit because the water has been taken out. For example, 2 tablespoons of raisins has 4 teaspoons of sugar; about the same amount of sugar as 1/2 cup of grapes.

Many of the *Meals for Good Health* lunches and dinners have two or more vegetables. This may be more than you are used to eating. It is an important change. Most of the breakfasts in *Meals for Good Health* have fruit. Fruit is often the dessert for lunch or dinner.

When you are hungry between meals, eating a vegetable or a fruit would be better than eating a high-fat snack food or a rich dessert. Low-fat starch foods are also good for snacks.

Vegetables & Fruits

Choosing Milk & Calcium-Rich Foods

Calcium is found in milk and foods made from milk.

Calcium is important for adults as well as for children.

Calcium is a mineral that makes your bones and teeth strong. It is found in milk and foods made from milk, such as yogurt and cheese. Calcium is also found in other foods, such as dried beans and a few other vegetables.

Infants and growing children need lots of calcium as their bones and teeth grow. Many people believe that milk and other calcium foods are just for kids. The truth is, we need calcium all our adult life to keep our bones strong.

Does drinking milk give you stomach pains? If so, you may not be able to fully digest the natural sugar (lactose) in the milk. You may be able to digest just small amounts of milk and foods made from milk, such as cheese or yogurt. You could also drink lactose-reduced skim milk which can be bought in large food stores.

You can also get your daily calcium from other foods, such as:

- tofu made with added calcium
- soy drinks made with added calcium
- beans, such as baked beans
- seeds and nuts, such as almonds and sesame seeds
- fish bones, such as those in canned salmon
- dark green, leafy vegetables, such as broccoli, Brussels sprouts, okra, kale and Chinese cabbage
- a few fruits, such as dried figs and oranges

Choose low-fat, calcium-rich foods, such as:

- low-fat milk, low-fat yogurt (skim or 1 percent) and low-fat cheeses (less than 20 percent milk fat)
- skim milk powder
- salmon canned in water, not oil
- low-fat soy milk
- dark green, leafy vegetables and beans are naturally low in fat

Seeds, nuts and tofu have vegetable fat; they can be chosen in the amounts suggested in the *Meals for Good Health* meals.

Most of the meals in *Meals for Good Health* include one or more calcium-rich foods.

Calcium-Rich Foods

Eating the Right Amount of Protein

You need only a small amount of protein each day.

Proteins are important to keep you healthy. However, we only need a small amount of protein every day. The *Meals for Good Health* meal photographs show you how much protein to eat.

You can easily get protein from animal foods, such as meat, eggs and milk. Proteins are also found in nuts, seeds, and many vegetables and grains. I have included a variety of vegetable and animal proteins in the *Meals for Good Health* meals.

Vegetable proteins
Kidney beans, brown beans, chickpeas and dried peas are low-fat vegetable proteins. Tofu is made from soy beans and can replace meat. Smaller amounts of vegetable protein are found in starch foods, such as whole wheat bread and oatmeal.

Nuts, including peanuts or peanut butter, and seeds, such as sunflower seeds, are high-fat vegetable proteins. They can still be a good choice for some meals, in the right amounts.

Animal proteins
Lean red meats are a good choice for low-fat animal protein. They include lean hamburger, round roast or steak, loin pork chop, and deer or rabbit. Chicken and turkey are a good source of protein, but remember to remove the skin.

Eggs are a good source of protein. Do you ask, "Can I eat eggs with high blood cholesterol?" Yes, you can safely eat three eggs a week. There are other important ways to reduce your high blood cholesterol (see page 39).

Most fish with the skin taken off has less fat than red meat. Some of the best low-fat fish are pike, pickerel, ocean perch, red snapper, cod, haddock and sole. Tuna, pink salmon and sardines canned in water are good choices too. Shrimp and lobster are also low in fat. Blue fish is a medium-fat fish. The fattier fishes are lake trout or red (sockeye) salmon; eat smaller portions of these.

Meats and Other Proteins

Choosing Fiber

Fiber is in:
- *Starch foods*
- *Vegetables*
- *Fruits*

The natural way to be regular is to eat high-fiber foods, drink lots of water and exercise.

One question I ask my clients is whether they are often constipated. It is a personal question, but it can tell me what they eat. Being regular depends so much on what you eat. People who eat many high-fiber starch foods, vegetables and fruits do not usually become constipated.

If you are sometimes constipated, you should know that you can be regular without laxatives. If you have been taking laxatives often or for a long time, this may have caused you to get a lazy bowel.

You can be regular without using laxatives.

Start eating more high-fiber foods. Add these high-fiber foods to your diet slowly so that you won't get cramps and gas. Drink lots of water. Go for walks. Your bowel muscles will get stronger and start to work for you again. As you make these changes over the next few months, you may not need a laxative at all.

Eat More Fiber Foods

Getting All Your Vitamins & Minerals

Spend your money on healthy foods instead of vitamin and mineral pills.

Vitamins and minerals are found in all foods. Extra vitamins and minerals have been added to many foods, such as breads, cereals and milk. By eating a variety of healthy foods, as shown in this book, you will get the vitamins and minerals that your body needs. These foods will help keep you healthy and reduce your chance of becoming ill.

You only need tiny amounts of vitamins and minerals to keep you healthy. For example, you need about 30 milligrams of Vitamin C every day. One orange has about 60 milligrams of Vitamin C. If you also take a pill of 1000 milligrams (or 1 gram) of Vitamin C every day, your kidneys have to work harder to flush out the extra Vitamin C.

Your healthy body looks after you, storing the vitamins and minerals that you need for later. For example, Vitamins A, D and E and iron are stored in your fat and liver. If you take these vitamins or minerals as pills, your body may end up with more than you need.

You do not need to take vitamin and mineral pills unless your doctor or dietitian has prescribed them. If a vitamin or mineral pill is prescribed for you, be sure to ask why, and know how many you should take.

Limiting Sugar, Salt & Alcohol

Limiting sugar

Sugar is found naturally in fruits, vegetables and even milk. The sugar in these foods gives you energy. These foods also have many other nutrients.

We need to limit pure sugars—white sugar, brown sugar, icing sugar, corn syrup, maple syrup, molasses and honey. One type of pure sugar is not better or worse than another. These pure sugars give us calories we don't need and very little nutrition. Such sugars are called "empty calories."

Sugars are added to most of our processed foods. In fact, it is hard to find a food label without sugar on the ingredient list. If sugar is the first ingredient, it means the food has more sugar than anything else. Try to limit foods that have a lot of added sugar.

Low-Calorie Sweeteners

Instead of sugar you may want to try using low-calorie sweeteners in your coffee, tea or on your cereal. Some common brand names are Equal (Nutrasweet), Splenda, Sugar Twin and Sweet N' Low. Low-calorie sweeteners have a lot less sugar and fewer calories than real sugar. Because these sweeteners have few calories, three or four packages (or teaspoons) a day would have little effect on your weight or blood sugar level. Foods that have low-calorie sweeteners added include diet soft drinks, light puddings, light gelatin and sugar-free gum.

One teaspoon of sugar has the same sweetness as 1 teaspoon of Splenda or 1/2 teaspoon of Sugar Twin or Sweet N'Low. If you find these sweeteners "super sweet," use a little less.

Different cereals have different amounts of sugar:

Bran Flakes – have a small amount of sugar added (1 teaspoon or 4 grams in 3/4 cup).

Frosted Flakes – have a large amount of sugar added (3 teaspoons or 12 grams in 3/4 cup).

*Sorbitol and fructose are **not** low-calorie sweeteners.*

You may see words such as sucrose, fructose, sorbitol and mannitol on food labels. Sucrose and fructose are pure sugars and they are not low-calorie. Sorbitol and mannitol are sweeteners that have slightly fewer calories than sugar and they raise the blood sugar more slowly.

Remember when we went on the shopping tour? We looked at some cookies, candies and chocolates that were made with sorbitol or mannitol and often found them to be high in fat. The sorbitol in them can also affect your weight and blood sugars. These foods are often not low-calorie. In fact, they may have similar calories to the regular cookies, candies or chocolates. Limit all of them.

Low-sugar baking tip:

When making your favorite recipe for muffins, cookies or cakes, cut the sugar in half. This reduced amount of sugar will still be enough for them to rise nicely. If you feel that your recipe is not sweet enough, you can add some low-calorie sweetener, such as Splenda or Sugar Twin. Sweeteners that have Nutrasweet, such as Equal, shouldn't be used for baking; they lose their sweetness when cooked.

Lots of sugar can be found in what you drink. High-sugar drinks include chocolate milk, milk shakes, fruit drinks, fruit crystal drinks, fruit juice and regular soft drinks. One cup of unsweetened fruit juice or 1 cup of regular soft drink has about 7 teaspoons of sugar. Choose water or diet drinks instead.

In a few *Meals for Good Health* dessert recipes sugar is used instead of fat. Sugar has fewer calories than fat. In the same way, small amounts of jam or syrup are included in some breakfasts, in place of margarine. This amount of sugar is part of a healthy diet, even if you have diabetes (see pages 39-41 to learn more about diabetes).

When you start choosing low-fat foods and eating fewer processed foods, you will be eating less fat and sugar.

You are on your way to losing weight.

Limiting salt

Salt gives us sodium, an important mineral. Sodium occurs naturally in foods. You need only a small amount of sodium for good health.

You only need a small amount of salt.

Unfortunately, most of us get more sodium than we need. We eat too many salty processed foods and many of us add too much salt to our food. This extra salt in our diet makes extra work for your kidneys.

Salt is added to a lot of foods.

Cutting back on salt is a good healthy change for everyone. If you have high blood pressure, cutting back on salt may help reduce your blood pressure. For some people with high blood pressure, however, making other changes including losing weight, exercising and quitting smoking (see page 39) may be more helpful.

Cutting back on salt means shaking a little less salt on your food, adding less salt (or no salt) to your recipes and limiting salty foods.

Once you start to cut back on salt, you will notice that many foods begin to taste too salty.

Try these tips to cut back on salt:

- Season your food during cooking and at the table with spices and herbs, lemon juice, lime juice or vinegar. Use lots of pepper instead of salt.
- Use garlic powder or onion powder instead of garlic salt or onion salt.
- Use less salt in cooking and baking. For many recipes you don't need to add any salt.
- Look for low-sodium or unsalted foods, such as unsalted soda crackers.
- Eat less take-out and restaurant meals. They are high in salt and fat.

Salt in *Meals for Good Health* recipes:

- Salt is not added to the recipes unless needed for rising or recipe quality.
- The flavor of some of the recipes is brought out by the use of dried bouillon powder or dried soup mix. Both bouillon powder and soup mixes are salty. If you need to cut out more salt, use less bouillon powder or soup mix and more spices and herbs. You can also buy reduced-salt bouillon powder.

Salt in *Meals for Good Health* meals:

- The meals in this book will help you cut back on salt.
- Some salty foods, such as dill pickles, sauerkraut, sausages and wieners are part of the meals. In the portions shown, these can be part of a healthy diet. If you need to cut out more of your salt, then you could choose sliced cucumber instead of a dill pickle, plain cabbage instead of sauerkraut, and unsalted beef or pork instead of sausages or wieners.

One beer or two ounces of hard liquor, such as whiskey or rum, have about the same number of calories as two slices of bread.

Six beers have 900 calories. That's a lot. Six diet soft drinks have only 20 calories.

Limiting alcohol

If you want to lose weight, you must look at everything you eat and drink, including alcohol. **Alcohol is high in calories.** Like sugar, alcohol is full of "empty calories." In this book you will find a glass of wine as an option with one of the meals. A light beer and shot of whiskey are shown in the snack photographs as occasional choices only.

The calories in hard liquor, such as whiskey, come from the alcohol alone. Three-quarters of the calories in beer comes from the alcohol with the rest coming mostly from sugar. In liqueurs, just over half the calories come from alcohol and the rest come from sugar.

To reduce calories from alcoholic drinks:

- Drink less beer, wine, liqueurs and hard liquor. Instead drink water, diet beverages, no-alcohol low-calorie beer, or coffee or tea.
- Choose a light or extra light beer, which has less sugar and less alcohol than regular beer.
- Instead of drinking a whole beer, have just half a beer and mix it with diet ginger ale.
- Most of the no-alcohol beers and no-alcohol wines have sugar (though usually less sugar than soft drinks) but are still a better choice than beer that has alcohol.
- If you want to have a glass of wine, choose dry wine. This has less sugar than sweet wine.
- Avoid liqueurs, which are heavy on alcohol and sugar.
- If you choose to have a drink of hard liquor, mix it with a diet soft drink or water instead of juice or regular soft drinks.
- Drink water before and with your meals, instead of alcohol. Alcohol often makes you feel hungrier.

Caution:

- *Alcohol does not mix well with some pills–check the pill bottle label to see if it is okay to drink alcohol.*
- *If you have diabetes and take insulin or diabetes pills, drinking alcohol can cause a low blood sugar reaction. To avoid this problem, don't drink, or limit your drinks to one or two; and never drink on an empty stomach.*

Alcohol is more than just a source of calories, it is an addictive drug. If you drink a lot of alcohol, it will be affecting more than your weight. Alcohol will make it hard to make other changes in your life.

Drinking less alcohol is a difficult choice but it's okay to ask for help.

Think about making a change.

Walking for Health

To lose weight, you need regular exercise.

Walking is the best exercise for most of us.

Three important things you will learn from this book are to eat less food, eat less fat and exercise more. It is a dream to think you can lose weight without regular exercise.

Walking is one of the best kinds of exercise. You can walk when you want and where you want. Start off slowly and try walking a little faster and farther each week.

Most of the people I counsel say they are active. I tell them that there is a difference between being active (or busy) and exercising. I compare the way we live today with the lives of our grandparents. People used to walk to work, to the store, to the post office, to school, to church and to the dance hall. Working in the home and on the farm was a lot of hard exercise. Today, we don't walk enough. We sit or stand for hours a day, whether at home or at work. This lack of exercise makes us unhealthy.

*You will find that exercise **gives** you more energy.*

Are you simply too tired to go for a walk? When your muscles are weak, you will feel tired. If you are overweight, going for a walk may even hurt. It may seem strange, but the only way to have the energy for walking is to go for a walk. Once you become more fit, you will find that walking gives you energy.

Are you so busy you can't find the time to go for a walk? Finding the time for a walk means making a few changes. Think about how often you go outside to do something—such as start the car or go to the bus stop, or get the mail. Once you are outside, take an extra twenty minutes to go for a walk. Walking is an important part of keeping healthy. We usually can find the time to do things which we think are important.

Walking can help you lose weight. It can also help you look and feel better. Walking keeps your bones and muscles strong. You will breathe deeper and easier. Walking often reduces back pain and other joint pain. Walking can help you reduce your stress and help you sleep better at night.

Walking helps you lose weight and helps in many other ways.

If you have diabetes, walking helps you lower your blood sugar. If you have high blood cholesterol, walking helps you lower your blood cholesterol. If you have high blood pressure, walking will help bring it down.

When I see a client two months after they have started walking, they tell me they feel healthier. They have often lost weight. They are now ready to do more walking, as it gets easier with each passing day.

It may take many months to get into a pattern of regular walking. Once you start walking more, you will feel better about yourself.

Put this book down and go for a walk.

Here are some helpful walking tips

First, start walking more each day.

When you go shopping, park at the far end of the lot and walk. When you take the bus, get off one stop early and walk that extra block.

Walking up and down stairs is great exercise. Start by walking down stairs.

Comfortable shoes or boots which fit well are important.

Then, start walking as a regular exercise.

Try to go for a walk twice a week. It may help to walk at the same time each day so it becomes a habit—a good habit. Your dog would love to go for a walk any time. Watching TV wastes a lot of good walking time.

Mark your calendar each day you go for a walk.

Boldly mark your calendar after each walk, and feel proud of yourself.

Next, walk farther. Walk more often. Walk faster and swing your arms.

Walk faster and you will lose more weight.

You may also want to swim, bike or do other exercises.

Now that you are walking, you may decide to also do some swimming, biking or dancing. An exercise bike or a treadmill can be used during those long winters. Good for you, if you start getting involved in other sports and activities.

Walking takes time, but it gives you a lifetime of better health. Enjoy!

Advice for Those with Diabetes or Heart Disease

The meal plans in *Meals for Good Health* will help you if you have diabetes. If you have heart disease, including high blood cholesterol, high triglycerides (blood fat) or high blood pressure, the meal plans are also suitable for you.

The advice for those of you with diabetes and heart disease is much the same as for all Canadians:

- lose weight if you are overweight
- eat a diet lower in fat, salt, sugar and alcohol
- eat a diet higher in starches, vegetables, fruit and fiber
- do not smoke
- exercise
- learn to relax
- take your pills and/or insulin as advised by your doctor
- have regular medical check-ups

The diet advice given by the Heart and Stroke Foundation of Canada and the Canadian Diabetes Association is similar to the advice you will find in ***Meals for Good Health.***

If you have heart disease:

If you have high blood pressure, a doctor or dietitian may advise you to limit salt. As a dietitian, I know that it is not just salt that raises blood pressure. To lower blood pressure, it is also important to make the other changes listed above. These changes are also important for lowering blood cholesterol.

High triglycerides (blood fat) are often caused by high blood sugar. This is because some of the extra sugar in your blood is changed into blood fat. Another possible cause of high triglycerides is drinking too much alcohol—alcohol can also be changed into blood fat. If your triglycerides are high, you should take steps to bring down your blood sugar and to cut back or stop drinking alcohol.

If you have diabetes:

Eating less fat is important when you have diabetes or heart disease.

If you have diabetes, eating too much fat may be more of a problem than eating too much sugar. If you are overweight and you lose body fat, this will make your insulin work better and your blood sugar will improve. Walking and other exercise will also make your insulin work better and will bring down blood sugar levels.

As a person with diabetes, you are more likely to have heart problems. If you eat less fat and walk, this will be better for your heart. The advice for heart disease and diabetes are much the same—eat less fat, lose weight and exercise more.

It is also important to eat regular small meals, as shown in this book, rather than just one large meal a day. This helps to even out your food and sugar over the day, so you can control your blood sugar better.

Small amounts of sugar can safely be eaten by a person with diabetes.

The advice from the Canadian Diabetes Association has changed in recent years. The Canadian Diabetes Association has a new food group called the Sugars group. It is now known that if you have diabetes, you can safely eat small amounts of sugar in the form of table sugar or candy. Of course, if you eat a large amount of a sweet food, you will have a quick and large rise in your blood sugar.

The total amount of carbohydrate in the meals can vary up to 2 Starch Choices (equal to about 2 slices of bread). You can talk to a dietitian or refer to the Manual (see page 232) to learn the exact amount of carbohydrate in each meal.

The meal plans in *Meals for Good Health* can safely be followed, even if you are taking insulin or diabetes pills. This is because the amount of carbohydrate (starch and sugar) in each meal is reasonable. There is some variation in the carbohydrate content of the meals and snacks, although the calories are the same. You may wish to order the *Meals for Good Health Manual* (see page 232) which lists the exact amount of carbohydrate in all the meals and snacks.

The *Meals for Good Health Manual* also lists the Canadian Diabetes Association's Food Choices and Food Symbols (see side bar) for all the meals, recipes and snacks shown in this book. This would be useful if you want more details about the nutrient content of the meals and snacks. **To learn how to get this manual see page 232.**

Canadian Diabetes Association
Food Choices and Food Symbols:

- ■ Starch Foods
- Fruits & Vegetables
- ◆ Milk
- ✱ Sugars
- Protein Foods
- ▲ Fats & Oils
- ++ Extras (low-calorie foods)

You may see these on food labels. They will tell you what kinds of food are in the product.

Read this if you are on diabetes pills, insulin, heart pills or blood pressure pills

- When you make changes, such as eating less or exercising more, you may not need as many pills or as much insulin. If you feel weak, shakey or dizzy when exercising, before meals or when getting out of bed, your pills may be too strong for you. See your doctor if you are not feeling well. Do not change your pills or insulin without talking to your doctor first.

- Ask your doctor or the pharmacist about what may happen if you drink alcohol when you are taking insulin, diabetes pills or heart pills.

If you are lean and do not need to lose weight
If you do not need to lose weight, you may wonder if you can still use this book. The answer is yes! Many changes that help a person lose weight, such as eating less fat and eating more fiber, are healthy changes for all of us. We all need different amounts of food. Pages 47-49 will help you choose the right size meals and snacks.

You are doing great. Making changes takes time and effort—but you are worth it!

Meals, Recipes and Snacks

Opening Words

About the meals

In this second part of the book you will find fifty meals. There are thirty-one dinner meals—one for every day of the month, if you wish. There are also nine breakfast meals and ten lunches.

The actual-size photograph shows the large meal.

For each meal there are two photographs. The photograph that is ***actual-size*** shows the large meal. The small meal is shown in the small inset photograph. The meals are made up of the same foods, but the portions are different. Take a look at Breakfast 4 on page 58-59. You will find the large meal shown actual-size and the small meal shown as an inset photograph on the top right-hand side of the page. Now look at Dinner 1 on pages 94-97. The large meal is shown in the actual-size photograph and the small meal is shown as an inset on the bottom left-hand side of the page.

Pages 47-49 will help you decide whether you should be choosing the large meals or the small meals.

On the page before each meal photograph, you will find a meal menu. This meal menu will show you the weight or size of the food portions that are in the photographs. For example, look at the bottom of page 58 and you will see the menu for Breakfast 4.

You can mix the order of the meals. For example, on Monday you may choose Breakfast 1, Lunch 4 and Dinner 8. If you like to eat your dinner at noon, then eat the lunch meal in the evening.

There are several meals in *Meals for Good Health* that you might eat in a restaurant. You will see from the photographs how much pizza, french fries or Chinese food you should order when you eat out.

Leftovers can be frozen to be eaten later or safely kept in your fridge for three days. I always try to have a couple of dinner meals in my freezer. I use these frozen meals when I'm short of time or when I don't feel like cooking.

Few of the meal photographs in *Meals for Good Health* show water, coffee or tea. Drink water with every meal and feel free to have coffee or tea. Don't forget to cut back, or cut out, added sugar and cream.

About the recipes

You will find sixty family-favorite recipes in *Meals for Good Health*. Most of the recipes use everyday foods. The recipes are easy to makc, nutritious and tasty. They use little added fat and most use little sugar. Salt is included as an option in some of my recipes; you can omit it if you wish.

This book has sixty recipes that are:
- *easy to make*
- *low-cost*
- *low in fat, sugar or salt*
- *family favorites*
- *easy to freeze*

If you live on your own, you may want to cut the recipes in half. Check the recipes for the number of servings. Some recipes will serve up to six. If you are cooking for a large family, the recipes can be doubled.

About the snacks

Following the dinner photographs, you will find a section on snacks. You will find more information about snacks on page 220-221.

About the weights and measures used in the recipes, meals and snacks

Standard measures are used in the recipes. If you want to use metric measures, here are the changes:

1 cup (8 ounces)	=	**250 milliliters (mL)**
1/2 cup (4 ounces)	=	**125 mL**
1/3 cup (3 ounces)	=	**80 mL**
1/4 cup (2 ounces)	=	**60 mL**
1 tablespoon	=	**15 mL**
1 teaspoon	=	**5 mL**
1 ounce	=	**28 grams**
1 pound	=	**454 grams**

Note:

- *There are 3 teaspoons in every tablespoon.*
- *There are 4 tablespoons in 1/4 cup.*
- *There are 16 tablespoons in 1 cup.*

Check how much your glasses and bowls hold

Your drinking glasses and cereal and soup bowls may be different shapes than the ones shown in the meal photographs. Fill up a measuring cup with water and pour the water into your glasses and bowls. Then you will know how much they hold.

Choosing the Right Size Meals & Snacks

Look at both the large and small photographs. Choose the meal size that has a little less food on the plate than you usually eat. Eating less will help you lose weight or stay at a healthy weight.

As you get older, you need smaller meals and fewer snacks.

If you are a senior and are overweight, perhaps you are eating the same amount of food as you did when you were younger. But you are probably less active than when you were younger. To lose weight slowly, all you may need to eat is the small breakfast, lunch and dinner, with no snacks. This will give you about 1,200 calories a day. If you added two small snacks to the three small meals, you would get another 100 calories. Different meal plans are shown in the table on page 49.

Do the large meal portions seem more reasonable to you? If so, choose three large meals with no snacks and you will get about 1,600 calories. The largest meal plan would be the three large meals with three large snacks—that would give you about 2,200 calories.

Cut back on your meals and snacks so that you lose weight slowly. It is not healthy to lose weight too quickly. Losing three or more pounds a week is not healthy because you will lose important muscle tissue as well as fat.

Losing weight slowly will help you keep the weight off. If you lose one or two pounds a month, you are doing well.

Meals for Good Health has been written for adults wishing to lose weight or stay at a healthy weight. Since the meals are nutritious, they are also healthy for your family, but the portions may need to be adjusted.
The small meals would be enough for most younger children. But growing children and teenagers may need portions larger than even the large meals and large snacks. For children and teenagers, include a cup of milk with each meal to meet their calcium needs. Replace the alcohol choices with non-alcohol drinks.

The calories are counted for you.

You don't need to worry about counting calories because I've worked it all out for you. If you eat the same size meals and snacks every day you will always get the same number of calories. The amount of starch, sugar, protein and fat is also fairly similar from meal to meal.

For the small meals:

- breakfast has 250 calories
- lunch has 400 calories
- dinner has 550 calories

For the large meals:

- breakfast has 370 calories
- lunch has 520 calories
- dinner has 730 calories

Think about this:
- *Three large snacks in a day adds up to 600 calories.*
- *Three small snacks in a day adds up to just 150 calories.*

For the snacks:

- a low calorie snack has 20 calories or less
- a small snack has 50 calories
- a medium snack has 100 calories
- a large snack has 200 calories

Daily calorie totals of different size meals (breakfast, lunch and dinner) and snacks:

• small meals with no snacks	1,200 calories
• small meals with two small snacks	1,300 calories
• small meals with one small snack and two medium snacks	1,450 calories
• small meals with one small, one medium and one large snack	1,550 calories
• large meals with no snacks	1,620 calories
• large meals with two small snacks	1,720 calories
• large meals with one small and two medium snacks	1,870 calories
• large meals with one small, one medium and one large snack	1,970 calories
• large meals with three large snacks	2,220 calories

Breakfast Meals

BREAKFAST 1 *Dry Cereal*

This is the easiest breakfast to prepare.

Look at the cereal labels before you buy. Choose cereals that have little or no added sugar. One serving should have less than 5 grams of sugar and less than 2 grams of fat.

If a cereal is made with added dried fruit, such as raisins, it will have a higher amount of sugar. For example, 1 tablespoon of raisins adds an extra 5 grams of sugar. If you are choosing a cereal with added fruit, you should have a smaller portion of fruit on the side.

Another thing to look for when you buy cereals is fiber. Cereals with a lot of fiber are a good choice. These would include bran cereals and whole wheat cereals.

Skim milk and 1 percent milk have very little fat, and are the best choice for your cereal and for drinking. If you use canned milk, buy skim evaporated milk. Remember, 1/4 cup evaporated milk mixed with 1/4 cup water is the same as 1/2 cup regular milk.

Add fruit to your cereal or eat it on the side. Choose a half a banana or any of the fruits you see with the other breakfast meals. A 1/2 cup of unsweetened juice has the same calories as one small fruit, but it does not have the fiber.

Drink water with all your meals, including breakfast. If you have a cup of coffee or tea, go easy on the sugar. Cut it out if you can, or use a low-calorie sweetener. Also, go easy on the cream and coffee whitener. You probably know that cream has a lot of fat, but did you know that coffee whitener is made mostly with sugar and oil? Instead of using cream or coffee whitener, try using skim milk or skim milk powder. If you want to use coffee whitener, buy the light kind and limit yourself to a couple of teaspoons a day.

Your Breakfast Menu	Large Meal	Small Meal
Bran flakes cereal Skim or 1 percent milk Half a small banana	1 1/4 cup 1 cup 3-inch piece	3/4 cup 1/2 cup 3-inch piece

Small Meal

BREAKFAST 2

Egg & Toast

Sugar, honey or jam has fewer calories than butter or margarine. This is because a gram of sugar has fewer calories than a gram of fat.

- *1 teaspoon of sugar, honey or regular jam or jelly has 20 calories.*
- *1 teaspoon of butter or margarine has about 40 calories.*

Large eggs have almost the same yolk size as small eggs. Large eggs are larger because they have more egg white. This means that a small egg has about the same cholesterol as a large egg.

If you want to fry your egg but don't have a non-stick pan, add a bit of water to your frying pan instead of adding fat.

For your toast, choose brown bread, such as whole wheat or rye bread. These breads have a lot of fiber.

For a light choice, put a small amount of jam or honey on your toast, without butter or margarine.

Boil an egg, or poach or fry it in a non-stick pan with no added fat.

A small serving of fruit or several slices of tomato goes with this meal. For a change, try 1/2 cup of tomato or vegetable juice. Tomato juice would be a light choice since it has half the sugar of fruit juice.

A note about fruit juice:
Fresh fruit is a better choice than fruit juice. This is because fresh fruit has more fiber and is more filling. However, you can choose 1/2 cup of unsweetened orange juice instead of one small orange.

Drink 1/2 cup of skim milk or 1 percent milk with this meal. One 1/2 cup of buttermilk is also low in fat.

Your Breakfast Menu	Large Meal	Small Meal
Egg (cooked without fat)	1	1
Brown toast	2 slices	1 slice
Margarine	2 teaspoons	1/2 teaspoon
Jam or jelly	1 teaspoon	1 teaspoon
Skim or 1 percent milk	1/2 cup	1/2 cup
Orange slices	1/2 a 3-inch orange	1/2 a 3-inch orange

Small Meal

BREAKFAST 3

Pancakes & Bacon

Look at the labels on light syrup. Two tablespoons should have fewer than 60 calories. Two tablespoons of this light syrup are the same as 1 tablespoon of most regular syrups.

For extra fiber, add 1 tablespoon of bran to your batter.

Try adding half an over-ripe, mashed banana into your pancake batter. It adds a nice flavor and sweetness.

If you don't have a non-stick pan, coat your frying pan lightly with a greased paper towel, or use a cooking spray.

These thin pancakes are easy to make. They are lower in fat and sugar than the store-bought pancake mixes.

Syrup replaces fruit in this breakfast.

Cook your bacon until crisp. Reduce the fat by draining off the grease. One thin slice of lean ham has less fat than bacon.

Low-Fat Pancakes

Makes sixteen 4-inch pancakes.

1 1/2 cups flour
1/2 teaspoon salt
1 teaspoon baking powder
1 tablespoon sugar
1 egg
1 tablespoon of oil, margarine or butter, melted
1 3/4 cups skim milk

1. In a large bowl mix together the flour, salt, baking powder and sugar.
2. In a medium bowl, beat the egg with a fork. Add the fat and milk to the egg, and mix well.
3. Add the egg mixture to the flour mixture. Stir until smooth. It helps to stir with a wire wisk. If it is too thick add a little more milk.
4. Cook on a non-stick pan, on medium heat or in an electric non-stick pan. Use about 3 tablespoons of batter for each pancake. Once the pancakes have small bubbles, turn them over.

Your Breakfast Menu	Large Meal	Small Meal
Low-Fat Pancakes	3	2
Syrup	1 1/2 tablespoons, or 3 tablespoons of light syrup	1 tablespoon, or 2 tablespoons of light syrup
Bacon, crisp	2 strips	1 1/2 strips

SMALL MEAL

BREAKFAST 4

Toast & Peanut Butter

• ***A*** *light (or "diet") jam or jelly should have fewer than 10 calories in 1 teaspoon (30 calories in 1 tablespoon). 2 teaspoons of this light jam are about the same as 1 teaspoon of regular jam or jelly.*

• ***Jams*** *marked "no sugar added" may in fact have added sugar in the form of concentrated fruit juice. These jams often have almost the same amount of sugar as regular jam.*

This simple breakfast has protein to start your day. One tablespoon of peanut butter is a good source of protein. But peanut butter has a lot of fat, so put it on a dry piece of toast—you don't need to add extra fat.

Half an apple is served with this breakfast.

Here are a few examples of other fruit servings:

- a half cup of unsweetened applesauce
- one large kiwi
- a quarter of a small melon
- a half a small banana
- one orange
- a half a grapefruit. See Breakfast 8 for a new way to enjoy grapefruit.

In place of the 1/2 cup of milk, you may have 1 cup of light hot cocoa (see Breakfast 9).

For the large meal, try the peanut butter on your first piece of toast and 1 teaspoon of jam or jelly on your lightly buttered second piece of toast.

Your Breakfast Menu	Large Meal	Small Meal
Brown toast	2 slices	1 slice
Peanut butter	1 tablespoon	1 tablespoon
Margarine or butter	1 teaspoon	–
Jam or jelly	1 teaspoon, or	–
	2 teaspoons diet jam	–
Skim or 1 percent milk	1/2 cup	1/2 cup
Apple slices	1/2 a 3-inch apple	1/2 a 3-inch apple

SMALL MEAL

BREAKFAST 5

Hot Cereal

Have only half a fruit serving if you choose to add 2 teaspoons of sugar:
- 1 tablespoon of raisins
- 1 prune
- 2 dried apple rings
- 1 dried apricot.

Have a full fruit serving of fruit if you don't choose sugar:
- 2 tablespoons of raisins
- 2 prunes
- 1/4 cup prune juice.

You may want to mix half a package of instant unsweetened oatmeal with half a package of one of the flavored oatmeals. This way you'll get a lightly sweetened oatmeal and you can add a half fruit serving.

Hot cereals such as porridge (oatmeal), whole grain cereals and corn meal cereal are high in fiber. Adding 1 tablespoon of wheat bran (or 1 teaspoon of flax seeds) to your hot cereal will give you even more fiber.

This breakfast has only half a fruit serving because 2 teaspoons of brown sugar (or white sugar or honey) are added to the hot cereal.

If you don't add any sugar to your cereal, or if you use a low-calorie sweetener, you may have a whole fruit serving (as shown with most of the other breakfasts).

Packaged single servings of oatmeal are fast and easy, but most have a lot of sugar added. Look for the ones that say "plain" or "natural" and check that sugar is not listed in the ingredients.

Your Breakfast Menu	**Large Meal**	**Small Meal**
Hot cereal	1 1/2 cups cooked (6 tablespoons dry)	1 cup (4 tablespoons dry)
Brown sugar	2 teaspoons	2 teaspoons
Raisins	1 1/2 tablespoons	1 tablespoon
Skim or 1 percent milk	3/4 cup	1/2 cup

SMALL MEAL
Winnipeg

BREAKFAST 6

French Toast

Two tablespoons of light syrup or 2 teaspoons of diet jam are the same as 1 tablespoon of regular syrup.

A pinch of nutmeg or cinnamon is a nice addition to the French toast dip.

French toast is quick and easy to make.

This breakfast is served with fruit and syrup. If you don't have fresh strawberries, any other kind of fruit, either fresh, frozen or canned, will do.

French Toast

Makes six pieces of toast.

2 large eggs

1/4 cup of skim milk

Pinch of salt, if desired

6 slices of bread

1. In a medium bowl, beat the eggs with a fork. Add the milk and salt.
2. Dip the bread into the egg and milk.
3. On a hot non-stick pan, cook both sides until golden brown. See page 56 if you don't have a non-stick pan.

Your Breakfast Menu	Large Meal	Small Meal
French toast	3 slices	2 slices
Jam	1 tablespoon, or 2 tablespoons diet jam	2 teaspoons, or 4 teaspoons diet jam
Strawberries	5 large	4 large

Small Meal

Breakfast 

Muffin & Yogurt

Large muffins, sold in donut shops, can have as much as five teaspoons of hidden fat. Try making these delicious, low-fat muffins. They only have 1/2 teaspoon of added fat in each muffin.

Instead of a muffin, you may have a low-fat granola bar.

Instead of yogurt, have a 1/2 cup of low-fat milk. For the small meal, you could have a slice of low-fat cheese instead of yogurt. See page 84, Lunch 7, to learn more about choosing yogurt.

Bran Muffins

Makes twelve medium muffins.

1 cup flour
1 1/2 teaspoons baking powder
1/2 teaspoon baking soda
1/2 teaspoon salt
1/4 cup unsweetened applesauce
2 tablespoons margarine
1/4 cup packed brown sugar
1/4 cup molasses (or honey)
1 egg
1 cup skim milk
1 1/2 cups wheat bran
1/2 cup raisins

1. In a medium bowl, mix flour, baking powder, soda and salt together.
2. In a large bowl combine applesauce, margarine and brown sugar. Stir with a wooden spoon until well mixed.
3. Beat in the molasses and the egg. Add the milk, then add the wheat bran.
4. Add the flour mixture to the large bowl. Then add the raisins. The mixture will be wet.
5. Spoon into an ungreased, non-stick muffin tin. If you don't have a non-stick tin, use paper cups or lightly grease your muffin tin. Bake in a 400°F oven for 20 to 25 minutes. They are ready when a toothpick put into the center of a muffin comes out clean.

Your Breakfast Menu	Large Meal	Small Meal
Bran Muffin	1	1
Low-fat fruit yogurt with low-calorie sweetener	1/2 cup	1/2 cup
Orange	1 small (2 to 3 inches)	1 small (2 to 3 inches)
Piece of cheese	1 ounce	–

SMALL MEAL

BREAKFAST 8

Raisin Toast & Cheese

Instead of two slices of raisin toast, you could have one raisin scone or one hot cross bun.

Instead of the cheese shown, you may choose a cup of milk.

A nice way to have grapefruit is to sprinkle it with a bit of cinnamon and low-calorie sweetener. Then, microwave it for thirty seconds or broil it until warm.

Raisin toast makes a nice change. You may want to have half your toast with the cheese broiled on top. The rest of the toast can be served with a thin spread of jam, which has fewer calories than margarine.

The large meal can include either 1 ounce of brick cheese or 1 1/2 slices of cheese. If you choose low-fat cheese, you will get less fat. Check the label:

- A low-fat block cheese or cheese slice has 20 percent or less milk fat (20% M.F.).
- Regular-fat cheese has about 35 percent milk fat.

Enjoy half a grapefruit or choose one serving of another type of fruit, such as:

- half a medium apple (or 1 small)
- a peach
- half a small banana
- an orange

Your Breakfast Menu	Large Meal	Small Meal
Raisin toast	3 slices	2 slices
Jam or jelly	1 teaspoon, or	–
	2 teaspoons of diet jam	–
Cheese slice	1 1/2 slices (1 ounce)	1 slice
Grapefruit	1/2	1/2

SMALL MEAL

BREAKFAST 9

Waffle & Hot Cocoa

Choose one of these instead of 1 cup of light hot cocoa:
- *1/2 cup low-fat milk*
- *1/2 cup diet yogurt*
- *1 slice (1 ounce) low-fat cheese*

Store-bought frozen waffles make an easy, quick breakfast. The plain waffles have fewer calories. For a treat, you may want to choose waffles that have blueberries or other fruits added.

Have your waffle with a small amount of jam, honey or syrup, as shown in the box below.

There is one fruit serving included with this breakfast.

Light hot cocoa mixes come in a variety of flavors. They are made with skim milk powder and are sweetened with a low-calorie sweetener. Choose a light hot cocoa mix that has fewer than fifty calories in a 3/4 cup serving. Check the label.

Your Breakfast Menu	Large Meal	Small Meal
Waffle	2	1
Margarine or butter	1 teaspoon	–
Syrup (or, honey or jam)	1 tablespoon, or 2 tablespoons light syrup	1 tablespoon, or 2 tablespoons light syrup
Grapes	3/4 cup	3/4 cup
Light hot cocoa	1 cup (14 g package)	1 cup (14 g package)

Small Meal

Lunch Meals

LUNCH 1

Sandwich with Milk

Here's a quick recipe for tuna or salmon filling. It makes enough for at least four sandwiches.

Mix together:

- *184 g can water-packed tuna*
- *1 tablespoon light mayonnaise*
- *1 tablespoon relish*
- *1 stick of finely chopped celery*

Don't put margarine or mayonnaise on your bread when you use this filling.

There are many nutritious fillings for sandwiches, for example, roast beef (as shown in the photograph), chicken, turkey, lean meat, cheese, egg or fish. Choose water-packed canned fish or leftover mashed fish for your sandwiches. Salmon and sardines are good choices because the fish bones give you calcium.

Each sandwich shown is made with 2 teaspoons of light mayonnaise. You may choose to use no fat at all, or use only 1 teaspoon of relish or mustard, or 1 tablespoon of salsa, which are all low in fat.

If you want a chopped filling, you can add celery, onion, green pepper or any other vegetable, with just a little light mayonnaise. Add your mayonnaise to the filling instead of on your bread.

Include some kind of vegetable on the side, such as three radishes, a stalk of celery, or a few slices of tomato or green pepper.

Cantaloupe or any other type of fruit serving is good with this meal.

You can have a cup of skim milk, 1 percent milk or buttermilk, or 3/4 cup of light yogurt. If you would like a slice of cheese as an extra in your sandwich, don't have the milk to drink.

Your Lunch Menu	Large Meal	Small Meal
Meat sandwich	1 1/2 sandwiches	1 sandwich
• bread, light rye	• 3 slices	• 2 slices
• roast beef	• 2 ounces	• 1 ounce
• light mayonnaise	• 1 tablespoon	• 2 teaspoons
• lettuce	• 2 large leaves	• 2 large leaves
Radishes	3	3
Cantaloupe	1/2 a small one	1/2 a small one
Skim or 1 percent milk	1 cup	1 cup

LUNCH 2

Beans & Toast

For a change, choose canned spaghetti instead of beans.

Open a can of brown beans, warm them up and serve a portion of them, as shown, with toast and fresh vegetables. Remove any chunks of pork fat from the baked beans, or buy beans canned only in tomato sauce.

For a change from toast, eat your beans with bannock (see page 115 for recipe) or another type of bread.

If you don't have any celery, choose a sliced tomato or 1/2 cup of tomato or vegetable juice.

Look for ice cream bars that are marked light or low-fat, and that are sweetened with a low-calorie sweetener. They taste good and have calcium. If you want to make your own low-fat and low-sugar frozen treats, try these Frozen Yogurt Bars.

Check the labels of light ice cream bars. Choose the ones that have fewer than 50 calories. One regular ice cream bar will have at least 150 calories.

One of these home-made Frozen Yogurt Bars has about 30 calories.

Instead of a light ice cream bar or home-made Frozen Yogurt Bar, you could have a 1/2 cup of milk.

Frozen Yogurt Bars

Makes eight bars.

2 cups plain skim milk yogurt

1/2 teaspoon diet (sugar-free) fruit flavored drink crystals

1. Mix the crystals with the yogurt.
2. Pour into containers and freeze.

Your Lunch Menu	Large Meal	Small Meal
Canned baked beans	1 1/4 cups	3/4 cup
Toast	2 slices	2 slices
Margarine	1 teaspoon	1 teaspoon
Celery sticks	2 stalks	2 stalks
Frozen Yogurt Bar	1	1

SMALL MEAL

LUNCH 3

Chicken Soup & Bagel

Grandmother was right. Chicken soup is good medicine when you are feeling ill; and when you are feeling well.

Although I do not add salt to this recipe, there is a lot of salt in the soup mix and bouillon. You may want to use a low-salt bouillon.

Instead of both salmon and cream cheese, a bagel could be served with any of these:

- *1 ounce or one thin slice of cheese or meat such as ham or turkey. Limit high-fat meats like bologna and salami.*
- *1/4 cup canned fish*
- *2 teaspoons peanut butter*

If you don't have bagels, you could make your sandwich with bread or a bun.

Canned soup or packaged soups are quick and easy. Add a handful of frozen vegetables for added nutrition. Cream soups have extra fat, so choose them less often. Try this recipe.

Chicken Rice Soup

Makes 7 1/2 cups.

2 medium carrots, chopped
1 medium onion, chopped
2 stalks of celery, chopped
1/4 cup rice (uncooked)
1 package (60 g) of dried chicken noodle soup mix
1 teaspoon (or half cube) chicken bouillon mix
1/4 teaspoon of dried dill
6 cups of water

1. Chop carrots, onion and celery.
2. Put all ingredients in a medium pot.
3. Cover and gently boil for about 20 minutes, until the carrots are cooked. Stir occasionally.

The bagel shown here is served with light cream cheese, and salmon, tomato and onion. For a change try smoked salmon (lox).

Your Lunch Menu	Large Meal	Small Meal
Chicken Rice Soup	1 1/2 cups	1 1/2 cups
Soda crackers	2	2
Bagel	1	1/2
Light cream cheese (20% fat)	1 tablespoon	1 tablespoon
Canned pink salmon	2 tablespoons	2 tablespoons
Tomato	1/2 a medium	1/2 a medium
Sliced onion	3 slices	3 slices
Orange	1 small (2 to 3 inches)	1 small (2 to 3 inches)

SMALL MEAL

LUNCH 4

Macaroni & Cheese

If you would like a slice of bread thinly spread with butter with this lunch, cut the macaroni and cheese by 1/4 cup.

If you don't have any green or yellow beans, choose raw vegetables such as:

- *up to three celery stalks*
- *one medium carrot*
- *one large tomato*
- *half a medium cucumber*

Boxed macaroni and cheese is an easy choice for lunch. After cooking the macaroni, just add milk and the powdered cheese. You don't need to add any butter or margarine.

For extra calcium, you can mix in 2 tablespoons of skim milk powder with the macaroni and cheese.

If you would prefer a home-made macaroni and cheese, there is a recipe with Dinner 18.

Green or yellow beans can be fresh, frozen or canned. Steam or microwave vegetables, or very lightly boil them. Overcooked vegetables lose important vitamins and minerals as well as good flavor.

Your Lunch Menu	Large Meal	Small Meal
Macaroni & Cheese (no added fat)	1 cup	3/4 cup
Green beans	1 cup	1 cup
Green olives	3	1
Apple	1 (3-inch)	1 (3-inch)

SMALL MEAL

Toasted Cheese & Tomato Sandwich

Coleslaw from a restaurant or store-bought has a lot of fat in the dressing. Try this recipe for a delicious low-fat coleslaw.

Mayonnaise has about the same calories as margarine or butter. If you choose a light mayonnaise or calorie-reduced margarine, you will get one-third the calories, or less. These light brands will have fewer than 45 calories in 1 tablespoon.

If you don't have the time to make your own coleslaw, have half a cup of raw vegetables instead.

Coleslaw

Makes 6 1/2 cups.

4 cups shredded cabbage

4 medium carrots, grated

4 stalks of celery, finely chopped

1 small onion

3 tablespoons low-fat (light) mayonnaise

1 tablespoon sugar

1/4 cup vinegar

1/4 teaspoon garlic powder

Salt and pepper, to taste

1. Chop the cabbage in fine strips, grate the carrots, and finely chop the celery and onion. Mix these together in a large bowl.
2. In a small bowl, mix the mayonnaise, sugar, vinegar, garlic powder, salt and pepper. Add to the cabbage. Mix well.
3. Cover and put in the fridge. This will keep well for one week.

Your Lunch Menu	Large Meal	Small Meal
Toasted cheese & tomato sandwich	1 1/2 sandwiches	1 sandwich
• bread	• 3 slices	• 2 slices
• cheese	• 1 1/2 slices	• 1 slice
• tomato	• 1 large	• 1 medium
• mayonnaise	• 2 teaspoons	• 2 teaspoons
Coleslaw	1/2 cup	1/2 cup
Cherries	1/2 cup	1/2 cup
Skim or 1 percent milk	1/2 cup	1/2 cup

Small Meal

LUNCH 6

Cold Plate with Soup

The vegetable soup may be dried or canned. Dried soups usually have fewer calories than canned.

Soda crackers are very low in fat. They have little fat compared with snack crackers. Choose the unsalted soda crackers.

Shop for low-fat cheese:
- *1% cottage cheese*
- *block cheese that is 20% M.F. (milk fat) or less*

Instead of the small bun shown, you could have a slice of bread, half an English muffin, one small bran muffin, four melba toast or six soda crackers (plus the two with your soup).

If you don't usually eat cottage cheese, have a slice of hard cheese instead.

You may choose cucumber instead of a dill pickle.

Have a fruit serving with your cold plate, either fresh, frozen or canned (in water or juice).

Your Lunch Menu	Large Meal	Small Meal
Vegetable soup (packaged)	1 cup	1 cup
Soda crackers	3	–
Cold plate		
• 1 percent cottage cheese	1 cup	1/2 cup
• peaches	2 halves	2 halves
• dill pickle	1 medium	1 medium
• lettuce	5 large leaves	5 large leaves
• tomato	1 medium	1 medium
• green onions	4	4
• whole wheat bun (small)	1	1
• Arrowroot biscuits	2	2

Small Meal

LUNCH 7

Peanut Butter & Banana Sandwich

Yogurt Ideas:
- *Mix one container of plain skim milk yogurt with one container of regular fruit yogurt. It will then have 1 1/2 teaspoons of sugar in 1/2 cup.*
- *Make up your own fruit yogurt simply by adding fruit to a low-fat yogurt. Add a low-calorie sweetener if you like.*

I never seem to get tired of peanut butter and banana sandwiches.

Make each sandwich without margarine or butter, and with 1 tablespoon of peanut butter and half a banana.

Peanut butter also goes well with jam or honey. Limit the jam or honey to 1 teaspoon, or 2 teaspoons of diet jam. Still have half a banana or any other fruit choice on the side.

My dad's favorite Sunday lunch is a peanut butter and onion sandwich. If you like onions, use as many as you like on your peanut butter sandwich. Have a fruit on the side.

Choose vegetable juice and carrot sticks as shown, or other fresh vegetables.

Regular fruit-flavored yogurt has 3 teaspoons of sugar added in 1/2 a cup. Using a yogurt made with a low-calorie sweetener will cut out this extra sugar.

You may have either 1/2 cup of light yogurt or 1/2 cup of low-fat milk.

Your Lunch Menu	Large Meal	Small Meal
Peanut butter & banana sandwich	1 1/2 sandwiches	1 sandwich
• white bread	• 3 slices	• 2 slices
• peanut butter	• 1 1/2 tablespoons	• 1 tablespoon
• small banana	• 1/2	• 1/2
Carrot sticks	1 medium carrot	1 medium carrot
Tomato or vegetable juice	1/2 cup	1/2 cup
Low-fat yogurt (sweetened with low-calorie sweetener)	1/2 cup	1/2 cup

SMALL MEAL

LUNCH 8

Pita Sandwich

Hummus can be made by blending canned chick peas. You can also buy hummus as a dry mix; you need only to add water to the dry mix. Add lemon, garlic and spices, such as cumin, for best flavor.

Tahini is ground sesame seeds, which can be bought in a small can. It is usually found near the peanut butter on grocery shelves.

Stuff your pita with lots of vegetables and a little protein.

Try these vegetables in your pita:

- lettuce and tomatoes
- bean sprouts and alfalfa sprouts
- grated carrots
- chopped green pepper

Try one of these in your pita instead of the cheese and ham *(portions are for the large meal):*

- 1/2 cup water-packed tuna or salmon
- 3/4 cup 1 percent cottage cheese
- 1/3 cup chopped firm tofu
- 1/2 cup hummus
- 1 1/2 tablespoons sesame tahini spread
- 1 1/2 tablespoons peanut butter

Include milk or some other milk food, such as yogurt or a diet ice cream bar.

Your Lunch Menu	Large Meal	Small Meal
Pita	1 (6-inch)	1 (6-inch)
• lettuce	1/4 cup chopped	1/4 cup chopped
• tomato	1/2 a medium	1/2 a medium
• bean sprouts	1/4 cup	1/4 cup
• carrots	1/2 a small	1/2 a small
• green pepper	2 tablespoons chopped	2 tablespoons chopped
• ham, lean	1 ounce	1 ounce
• cheddar cheese, shredded	3 tablespoons	2 tablespoons
Plums	2 medium	1 medium
Skim or 1 percent milk	1/2 cup	1/2 cup
Gingersnap cookies	2	–

SMALL MEAL

Chef's Salad, Bun & Soup

When you order a salad in a restaurant, ask for low-fat salad dressing on the side. If you don't, your salad will come soaked in fat and will be just as greasy as your neighbor's order of fries. Many clients have told me that they enjoy their salad with vinegar or lemon juice.

Low-fat salad dressings should have fewer than 10 calories per tablespoon. Look for those that say "oil-free" or "fat-free". Regular salad dressings often have more than 100 calories per tablespoon.

In restaurants, salads often are served with greasy garlic toast. Ask for a plain bun or dried bread sticks instead.

Whether you're at home or in a restaurant, you may want to have a salad with a bun and soup for your lunch.

A chef's salad, Caesar salad or Greek Salad is easy to make. A chef's salad recipe follows, and there is a recipe for Greek salad on page 207. You can toss these salads with a store-bought oil-free dressing and low-fat croutons.

Chef's Salad

Makes two servings.

2 cups chopped lettuce

2 medium tomatoes, sliced

Other vegetables, such as onions, green peppers, celery, radishes or carrots

1 apple, sliced

2 slices of cheese or meat

2 eggs, hard boiled and sliced

2 tablespoons croutons

1. Toss vegetables and apple. Place the meat or cheese and egg on top.
2. Add a low-fat salad dressing and croutons.

Your Lunch Menu	Large Meal	Small Meal
Cream of celery or tomato soup (made with water)	1 cup	clear broth (optional)
Wheat crackers	2 halves	–
Chef's Salad	1 serving (half of recipe)	1 serving (half of recipe)
Low-fat salad dressing	1 tablespoon	1 tablespoon
Bun, white	1 small	1 small
Margarine	1/2 teaspoon	1/2 teaspoon

Small Meal

LUNCH 10

French Onion Soup

With the large lunch, the soup is served with a salad, a slice of rye bread (or a small bun) and a fruit.

Choose light bouillon for less salt, if you wish.

Another way to make this soup is to use one package of dried onion soup mix (the kind with dried flakes of onion). This package of soup would replace the bouillon and the onions.

Regular-fat cheese is used in this recipe—as low-fat cheese does not broil as nicely.

French onion soup is a meal all on its own. It's easy to make at home with this recipe.

Other hearty soups are canned split pea or bean soup, or home-made hamburger soup (see recipe on page 114). Or you could have a bowl of cream soup made with milk and toss in some vegetables.

French Onion Soup

Makes four servings.

4 packets (or 4 cubes) beef bouillon mix

4 cups water

2 medium onions, thinly sliced

4 slices white bread, toasted

4 ounces of Swiss or mozzarella cheese (this is equal to four slices of cheese, each 4-inch square and 1/8-inch thick)

1. Add the bouillon mix, water and sliced onions to a pot. Bring to a boil. Turn down heat and simmer for 15 minutes until onions are soft.
2. Pour soup into four oven-proof bowls.
3. Cut dry toast into cubes. Put one full slice of cubed toast onto each bowl of soup. Place a slice of Swiss cheese on top of the bread.
4. Broil in the oven until the cheese bubbles.

Your Lunch Menu	Large Meal	Small Meal
French Onion Soup	1 serving	1 serving
Tossed salad	large	large
Oil-free salad dressing	1 tablespoon	1 tablespoon
Rye bread	1 slice	–
Margarine	1 teaspoon	–
Pear	1	1

Small Meal

Dinner Meals

DINNER 1

Baked Chicken & Potato

It is important to remove the fatty chicken skin. Roll the chicken in a store-bought shake-and-bake coating, or sprinkle on this salt-free and sugar-free coating. Bake the chicken on a rack so the extra fat drip offs. Bake in a 350°F oven, or grill on the barbecue.

Chicken Spice Mix

Makes enough for many meals.

2 teaspoons oregano

1 teaspoon thyme

1 teaspoon paprika

1 teaspoon pepper

1 teaspoon chili

1. Put all the ingredients in a jar with a tight lid. Mix well.
2. Sprinkle the mixture on the skinless chicken.

Compare the fat and sugar content of fast-food chicken with this home-baked chicken, which has the skin and fat removed.

The breast of baked chicken shown in the **small** meal photograph has:

- 1 teaspoon of fat
- no sugar

The same piece of chicken, if battered and deep-fried at a fast-food restaurant, would have:

- 4 teaspoons of fat
- 3 teaspoons of sugar or starch

Have your potato plain, with 1 teaspoon of butter or margarine, or with 1 tablespoon of light sour cream.

The vegetables that go with this meal are celery, radishes and frozen mixed vegetables.

Instead of frozen mixed vegetables, you could choose one of these sweet vegetables:
- *peas*
- *carrots*
- *parsnips*
- *beets*
- *turnips*
- *squash (orange)*

Easy-to-make pudding from a box:
Light puddings sweetened with a low-calorie sweetener are a good source of calcium and have fewer calories than regular puddings. Make your puddings with skim milk. Butterscotch pudding has been chosen for this meal, but you can choose your own favorite flavor.

Store-bought light puddings or light mousses should have fewer than 75 calories in a 1/2 cup serving.

Instead of pudding, you could choose 1 cup low-fat milk.

Your Dinner Menu	Large Meal	Small Meal
Baked chicken	1 1/2 breasts (5 ounces, cooked)	1 breast (3 1/2 ounces, cooked)
Baked potato, with skin	1 large	1 medium
Light sour cream	1 1/2 tablespoons	1 tablespoon
Mixed vegetables	3/4 cup	3/4 cup
Radishes	3	3
Celery	1 stalk	1 stalk
Light butterscotch pudding	1/2 cup	1/2 cup

Small Meal

DINNER 2

Spaghetti & Meat Sauce

Whether you use regular or lean ground beef, it is important to brown it first and drain off as much fat as you can.

You can remove extra fat by adding hot water to the browned meat, then draining it off.

For a meatless spaghetti sauce, make this recipe but do not add the meat or the tomato paste. For protein for the large meal, sprinkle 5 tablespoons of shredded cheese or 3 tablespoons of sunflower seeds on top of your spaghetti and sauce. Use a little less for the small meal.

Store-bought spaghetti sauces (in jars or cans) can have a lot of added fat, sugar or starch. For example, one cup of some meatless spaghetti sauces have 2 teaspoons of added fat and 4 teaspoons of added sugar or starch. If you do buy spaghetti sauce, look for one labeled as light.

Spaghetti and meat sauce is an easy-to-make favorite. I often double this recipe and freeze the extra. When you have no dinner planned, it's great to have a container of spaghetti sauce in the freezer.

Spaghetti Meat Sauce

Makes six cups of sauce.

1 pound lean ground beef

1 medium onion

28 ounce (796 ml) can of tomatoes

1 cup water

1 small tin (156 ml) tomato paste

1/2 teaspoon garlic powder

2 bay leaves (remove before serving)

1/2 teaspoon chili powder

1 teaspoon oregano

1 teaspoon basil

1/4 teaspoon paprika

1/8 teaspoon cinnamon

1/8 teaspoon cloves

1 cup chopped vegetables, such as green pepper, celery or mushrooms

1. Brown the ground beef. Drain off as much fat as you can.
2. Add the rest of the ingredients.
3. Bring to a boil, then turn down heat. Cover and simmer for 2 hours. Stir every now and then so the sauce doesn't stick. Add extra water if it gets too thick.
4. Serve over hot spaghetti, with Parmesan cheese if you like.

Use regular or wholewheat spaghetti.
Add dry spaghetti to a pot of boiling water, stir and cook for about 10 minutes. Drain off water.

Carrots are served with this meal.

Use an oil-free salad dressing. See Lunch 9, page 88, for more about low-fat salad dressings.

Light gelatin has few calories and is a good dessert choice after a big meal. It takes only a few minutes to make, but must be left in the fridge for about two hours to set. If you find the boxed diet gelatins are costly, try this easy-to-make recipe.

Light Gelatin

Makes two cups.

1 envelope unflavored gelatin

1/2 package regular Kool-Aid or Freshie

1 cup cold water

1 cup boiling water

Low-calorie sweetener equal to 1/4 cup of sugar (use a bit less or more, to suit your taste)

1. Soften the unflavored gelatin in 1/2 cup cold water.
2. Add the Kool-Aid or Freshie and 1 cup boiling water. Stir until gelatin is all mixed in.
3. Add 1/2 cup cold water and low-calorie sweetener.
4. Chill until firm (about 2 hours).

Whipped Gelatin is a variation you may want to try (see Dinner 10, page 131). When you whip the gelatin, you will get 4 cups instead of 2.

Another low-calorie dessert is store-bought "No sugar added" popsicles.

Your Dinner Menu	Large Meal	Small Meal
Spaghetti	1 3/4 cups	1 1/2 cups
Meat sauce	1 1/4 cups	3/4 cup
Cooked carrots	1/2 cup	1/2 cup
Salad	medium	medium
Oil-free salad dressing	1 tablespoon	1 tablespoon
Skim or 1 percent milk	3/4 cup	1/2 cup
Light gelatin	1/2 cup	1/2 cup

SMALL MEAL

DINNER 3

Fish with Rice

Low-fat fishes include sole, pickerel, red snapper and haddock. Blue fish is a medium-fat fish. The high-fat fishes include trout and red (sockeye) salmon. Eat a bit less of the high-fat fishes.

These spices go well with fish:
- *allspice*
- *basil*
- *cajun spice*
- *curry*
- *dill*
- *mustard*
- *oregano*
- *parsley*
- *thyme*

One cup of cooked brown rice has 50 fewer calories than one cup of cooked white rice.

Soy sauce is a good low-fat topping for rice instead of butter or margarine.

For extra flavor, cook rice in part tomato juice, or add to the water one packet of bouillon mix (or one cube).

The fish may be broiled or baked in an oven at 350°F. The fish shown in the photograph is red snapper, and it was baked and lightly brushed with margarine. Fish can also be microwaved, steamed, grilled on the barbecue, or fried in a non-stick pan (with just a little fat). If you are cooking fish in your oven or on your barbecue, you can wrap it in tin foil. Fish is good with spices, onions and vegetables wrapped up in the foil too.

Before cooking fish:
Before cooking fish, poke it with a fork and pour 2 tablespoons of lemon juice or a 1/4 cup of dry wine over it. Sprinkle it with your favorite spices. You may also want to roll the fish in bread crumbs or flour.

The secret to great tasting fish is to not overcook it. Fish is cooked when it flakes easily.

Fish is good served with lemon or a bit of tartar sauce. It's nice with salsa sauce too.

Brown rice adds some color and fiber to this meal. Because of the extra fiber in brown rice, it has fewer calories than white rice.

Leftover brown or white rice can be used to make Rice Pudding (see Dinner 5, page 111, for the recipe).

How to cook rice:
Put rice in a heavy pot. Rinse once with water. Add enough water to cover by 1/2 inch. Bring the rice to a fast boil, then put on a tight lid and turn the stove down to the lowest heat. Cook white rice for twenty minutes and brown rice for forty minutes. Do not take the lid off while the rice is cooking. This way, your rice will always be moist and fluffy.

When you are in a hurry, you can use instant rice. It cooks in just 5 minutes.

This meal is served with peas, a sweet vegetable, and with yellow or green beans, which are less-sweet. For extra flavor without many calories, mix a small can of mushrooms in with the peas.

Enjoy a delicious fruit milkshake with this meal. This milkshake is easy to make. It is so thick and good, you won't believe it's made with skim milk and not with ice cream.

Other less-sweet vegetables are:
- *summer squash or spaghetti squash*
- *broccoli*
- *cauliflower*
- *spinach*

See page 131 for more.

Fruit Milkshake

Makes 2 cups.

1 cup skim milk

1/2 cup frozen or fresh fruit of your choice

1 tablespoon sugar or equal amount of low-calorie sweetener

1. Pour the milk in a mixing bowl or a blender. Place your mixing bowl or blender in your freezer for half an hour.
2. Take your bowl or blender out of the freezer. Add the fruit and sugar (or low-calorie sweetener) to the milk. Mix in the blender for about thirty seconds. If you don't have a blender, mix in your bowl with beaters until thick and frothy. Serve right away.

Turn to page 31 to learn how much low-calorie sweetener to use instead of sugar.

Your Dinner Menu	Large Meal	Small Meal
Fish with lemon slice	6 ounces, cooked	4 ounces, cooked
Margarine (to cook fish)	1 teaspoon	1 teaspoon
Brown rice	1 1/4 cups	3/4 cup
Green peas	1/2 cup	1/2 cup
Yellow beans	1 cup	1 cup
Fruit Milkshake	1 cup	1 cup
Kiwi	1 medium (3-inch)	1 medium (3-inch)

SMALL MEAL

DINNER 4

Roast Beef

The lower cost, medium-tender, low-fat cuts of roast beef are:
- *"round" cuts, such as inside round and outside round*
- *"loin" cuts, such as sirloin or sirloin tip.*

Roast beef can also be cooked in a table-top "slow-cooker" pot.

You can also buy low-fat gravy mix packages, to which you add only water. These should have fewer than 10 calories in a serving. Look for one that says it is low in calories; it may be called "au jus" (with juice).

Choose light bouillon cubes to reduce salt.

Do not use plain water for the 2 cups of liquid, or your gravy will taste plain.

Gravy Flavorings:
- *canned mushrooms*
- *hot sauce*
- *pepper*
- *Worcestershire sauce*
- *garlic*

Here's a great way to cook your roast:

- Place your roast on a rack in a roasting pan, with no lid. Add 1 cup of water to the pan. Sprinkle with pepper but not salt (salt tends to dry out the roast). Bake in a hot 500°F oven for 30 minutes.
- Reduce the oven heat to 275°F. Leave roast uncovered and cook for another 1 1/2 hours for a 5-pound (2.4 kg) roast.

Once the roast beef has been removed from the pan, skim the fat from the meat juice with a spoon. Or, put some ice cubes into the meat juice, and the fat will stick to the ice cubes. With a spoon, take out the ice cubes. If you have time, you can let the juice cool and the fat in the juice will harden and can then easily be removed. You can serve the meat juice as it is, or thicken it into a gravy as below.

Low-Fat Gravy

Makes 2 1/3 cups

2 packets (or 2 cubes) beef bouillon mix (use chicken bouillon if making gravy for poultry)

1 teaspoon onion soup mix (or 1 tablespoon finely chopped onion)

2 cups liquid made from either fat-free meat juice, potato water or other vegetable water

1/4 cup flour, cornstarch or instant blending flour

1/2 cup cold water

1. Add the beef bouillon and onion soup mix to your 2 cups of hot liquid.
2. In a jar, mix the flour with the cold water. Tighten the lid and shake well. Add this mixture slowly to the hot juice and cook at medium heat. Stir it often with a whisk until thick and smooth, about five minutes.

The oven-roasted potatoes are peeled and cooked for an hour on a non-stick or greased rack or pan. Coat your potatoes with an oil-free Italian dressing or sprinkle with spices.

Have beets as shown, or carrots, turnips, corn, peas, or any other vegetable.

For dessert have the rhubarb with either a lower-fat ice cream (made with 10 percent B.F., or butter fat), sherbet, frozen yogurt or ice milk. If you don't want dessert, drink a cup of milk with your meal.

Enjoy horseradish with your roast beef; it is a low-fat relish.

Vegetables such as carrots are also good baked on a rack in the oven.

Stewed Rhubarb

Makes 1 3/4 cups

4 cups rhubarb (fresh or frozen) 1-inch pieces

2 tablespoons water

1/2 teaspoon sugar-free drink mix (either strawberry or raspberry)

Dash of cinnamon

1. Put the rhubarb and water in a heavy pot and cook at low temperature on the stove. Add water as needed. Cook for about 15 minutes, or until soft.
2. Take off the stove and, while still warm, add sugar-free drink mix and cinnamon.
3. Have it warm or cool. Keep in the fridge.

This rhubarb is nice as a dessert or as a snack served warm on a piece of toast.

The low-calorie sweetener in the drink mix adds enough sweetness.

Your Dinner Menu	Large Meal	Small Meal
Roast beef	5 ounces, cooked	3 ounces, cooked
Horse radish	1 tablespoon	1 tablespoon
Baked (or pickled) onions	3 small or 1 medium	3 small or 1 medium
Roasted potatoes	1 large	1 medium
Low-Fat Gravy	1/4 cup	2 tablespoons
Beets	1/2 cup	1/2 cup
Salad	small	small
Oil-free Italian salad dressing	1 tablespoon	1 tablespoon
Stewed Rhubarb	1 cup	1 cup
Ice Cream	1/3 cup	1/3 cup

SMALL MEAL

DINNER 5

Dinner Cold Plate

This is one of my mom's favorite light meals. I like it because it's easy to make. It's great on a hot day when you don't feel like cooking.

Two ounces of regular fat cheese (32 percent fat) is about equal in calories to:
- *3 ounces of low-fat (17 percent fat) cheese*
- *1 1/4 cups of 1 percent cottage cheese*

You may wish to replace the cheese shown in the photograph with low-fat cheese (see side bar).

Fish choices include salmon, tuna, sardines, shrimp, crab or lobster, all canned in water. Red (sockeye) salmon is included with this meal. You may want to choose pink salmon, which is a bit lower in fat than red. You may have one slice of cold meat instead of fish.

Your starch may be a bun, two slices of bread, or eight melba toast.

Add any number and variety of fresh vegetables.

For dessert have this rice pudding. The pudding is not too creamy but has a nice cinnamon flavor and is the right sweetness. It is good warm or cold.

Rice Pudding

Makes 4 cups (eight servings).

1 egg

1 1/2 cups skim milk

2 tablespoons sugar (or low-calorie sweetener, if desired)

1/2 teaspoon cinnamon

1/2 teaspoon vanilla

2 cups cooked rice (brown or white)

1/4 cup raisins

Instead of the rice pudding you could have a light pudding, a small dish of sherbet or frozen yogurt, or a serving of fresh fruit.

1. In a large bowl, beat the egg, milk, sugar or sweetener, cinnamon and vanilla. Use a spoon or whisk.
2. Stir in rice and raisins.
3. Pour into lightly greased baking dish.
4. Bake at 350°F for forty-five minutes or until the center is set.

Your Dinner Menu	Large Meal	Small Meal
Dinner Cold Plate		
• lettuce	3 large leaves	3 large leaves
• tomato	1/2 medium	1/2 medium
• green & red pepper	5 rings	5 rings
• cucumber	4 thick slices	4 thick slices
• radishes	2 large	2 large
• red salmon, water-packed	1/2 cup	1/2 cup
• cheddar cheese	2 ounces	1 ounce
• bun, whole wheat	1	1
• margarine	1/2 teaspoon	–
Rice Pudding	1 cup	3/4 cup

SMALL MEAL

DINNER 6

Hamburger Soup & Bannock

The great thing about this soup is that it is a meal all in one. Freeze any leftovers.

Hamburger Soup

Makes 10 cups.

1 pound hamburger (or 1 pound chopped or ground wild meat)
1 medium onion, chopped
1 clove garlic or 1/4 teaspoon garlic powder
19 ounce (540 ml) can tomatoes
10 ounce (284 ml) can tomato soup
1 teaspoon Worcestershire sauce
1/8 teaspoon pepper
4 cups water
4 packets (or 4 cubes) beef bouillon mix
3 medium carrots, peeled and sliced
1 cup chopped cabbage
12 ounce (341 ml) can kernel corn
1/4 cup dry macaroni

1. Brown the hamburger meat. Drain off as much fat as you can.
2. Add the onions and garlic, and cook at low heat until onions are soft.
3. Add the tomatoes, tomato soup, Worcestershire sauce, pepper, water and bouillon mix.
4. Bring to a boil, cover and simmer for one hour.
5. Add the vegetables and macaroni. Cover and simmer for another one hour.

If you've never had bannock—try it. This bread is made without yeast and is easy to make. It is cooked in the oven or in a cast-iron frying pan. Instead of the piece of bannock shown here, you may choose two slices of bread or one bun.

Bannock

Makes one 9-inch bannock (or ten pieces)

3 cups flour

1 tablespoon baking powder

1 teaspoon salt

1 tablespoon sugar

1/4 cup margarine or other fat, melted

1 cup skim milk

1. In a large bowl, mix together the flour, baking powder, salt and sugar.
2. Mix the melted margarine with the milk. Add this mixture to the flour. Mix with a spoon to make a soft dough.
3. Put this on a floured board or table. With your hands, knead gently five times.
4. Put on a non-stick or lightly greased cookie sheet. Flatten and shape until it is one 9-inch piece. Bake in the oven at 375°F for twenty minutes, until lightly browned.
5. Cut into ten pieces.

You can use any type of fat when you make bannock. I prefer to use margarine because it gives the bannock a nice golden color.

I use milk instead of water in the bannock because the milk helps in the rising, adding flavor and good nutrition, too.

Here's how you can cook bannock on your stove or campfire. Make the bannock batter with only 2 tablespoons of margarine or other fat. Add an extra tablespoon of milk to keep the batter soft. Into the cast-iron pan, add 2 tablespoons fat and fry the bannock for ten minutes on each side at low heat. This fried bannock has the same amount of fat as it does when baked.

Bannock is nice when 1/4 cup of raisins or blueberries are added to the batter.

Your Dinner Menu	Large Meal	Small Meal
Hamburger Soup Bannock Margarine Orange	1 1/2 cups 2 pieces 1 teaspoon 1 large	1 1/2 cups 1 piece 1 teaspoon 1 large

Small Meal

DINNER 7

Beans & Wieners

For extra flavor, try adding one of these to your beans and wieners:

- *1 tablespoon salsa sauce*
- *1 teaspoon Worcestershire sauce*
- *1/4 teaspoon hot sauce*

Beef or pork wieners are high in fat and salt. This meal makes a few wieners go a long way. The beans are low-fat and give you protein and fiber.

Try a lower fat wiener such as a turkey wiener. A tofu wiener is a vegetarian choice and is even lower in fat. Tofu is made from soy beans, which are low in fat and high in protein. You will usually find tofu and tofu wieners in the vegetables section of your grocery store.

Beans and Wieners

Makes 2 1/4 cups

14 ounce (398 ml) can brown beans (in tomato sauce)

3 regular wieners

1. Place the beans in a pot or cooking dish.
2. Cut the wieners in slices and add to the beans.
3. Heat on the stove or in a microwave oven.

Serve Beans and Wieners with toast and a tossed salad, with chocolate mousse for dessert.

This dessert recipe is easy to make, and it is thick and delicious.

Chocolate Mousse

Makes six 1/2 cup servings.

1 package (4 servings) of light chocolate instant pudding mix

1 1/2 cups skim milk

1 cup frozen whipped topping, thawed until soft

1. Pour the 1 1/2 cups skim milk into a medium bowl and add the pudding mix. Beat with a whisk or an electric mixer until thickened (about two minutes).
2. Fold in the thawed whipped topping until well blended (or if you want a marbled look, fold in the topping gently and don't fully mix).
3. Pour into six dessert dishes, and serve.

You may want to make this chocolate mousse with regular pudding instead of light. By doing so, you will add an extra 2 1/2 teaspoons of sugar to each serving.

Your Dinner Menu	Large Meal	Small Meal
Beans & Wieners	1 1/2 cups	1 cup
Toast	2 small or 1 regular slice	2 small or 1 regular slice
Margarine	1/2 teaspoon	–
Tossed salad	large	large
Oil-free salad dressing	1 tablespoon	1/2 tablespoon
Chocolate Mousse	1/2 cup	1/2 cup

SMALL MEAL

DINNER 8

Steak & Potato

Look for "round" or "loin" cuts of beef. These are lowest in fat and are less costly.

Trim off all the fat.

On the barbecue, try not to let your meat burn. You can stop this by lightly spraying the coals with water to keep the flames down.

The simplest way to cook a steak is to barbecue or broil it, or fry it in a very hot, heavy frying pan with a bit of water. If frying in a pan, cover with a lid to reduce fat spraying out. Cook for only about four minutes on each side.

If you need your steak to be more tender, here are two more good ways to cook it:

- Soak it for a few hours in canned tomatoes, wine, wine vinegar, beer or plain yogurt. Then fry the steak in a bit of broth or water, or barbecue or broil it.
- Brown the steak on the stove in a bit of beef broth or water. Add one can of tomatoes or 1 cup of salsa. Cover the pan and simmer for an hour.

Fresh mushrooms can be barbecued or broiled. Canned or fresh mushrooms can be cooked in a separate pan or added to the pan with the steak.

Serve the steak with Low-Fat Mashed Potatoes or with a boiled or baked potato.

Low-Fat Mashed Potatoes

Make low-fat mashed potatoes by mashing the potatoes and adding only milk, no butter or margarine. Add enough milk to make the potatoes creamy and smooth.

Spice Mix

Here is a spice mix you can make. Shake some on your meat, your potato or rice, and your vegetable.

2 teaspoons garlic powder
2 teaspoons dried lemon powder
1 teaspoon basil
1 teaspoon oregano
1 teaspoon pepper
1 teaspoon chili

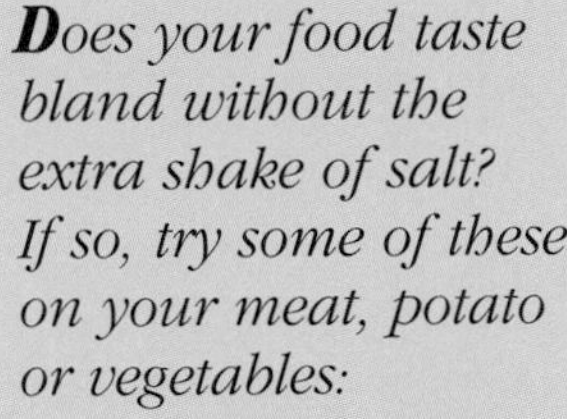

Does your food taste bland without the extra shake of salt? If so, try some of these on your meat, potato or vegetables:

- *pepper*
- *parsley, lemon or lime (fresh or dried)*
- *onion powder*
- *garlic powder*
- *spices or herbs*
- *store-bought spice mixes*

Choose an oil-free or fat-free salad dressing for your salad.

Brussels sprouts are healthy mini-cabbages. If you don't have any, choose one of your own favorite vegetables.

Sherbet, frozen yogurt, ice milk and 10% B.F. ice cream have less fat than regular ice cream.

Your Dinner Menu	Large Meal	Small Meal
Steak	5 ounces, cooked	3 ounces, cooked
Low-Fat Mashed Potatoes	1 cup	2/3 cup
Mushrooms	1/2 cup	1/2 cup
Brussels sprouts	3/4 cup	3/4 cup
Salad	large	large
Oil-free salad dressing	1 tablespoon	1 tablespoon
Sherbet	1/2 cup	1/2 cup

SMALL MEAL

DINNER 9

Cheese Omelet

You can add an extra egg white to your omelet. An egg white has no cholesterol and only 20 calories. An egg yolk has 60 calories.

Try this in your omelet:
- *a sprinkle of dried or fresh dill or parsley*
- *1 tablespoon of finely chopped onion, green onion or chives.*

An omelet makes a great dinner. I cook a cheese omelet about once a week because it is easy and fast. It is okay to have eggs for a main meal once a week, as long as the eggs are eaten in place of meat.

Cheese Omelet

This is the recipe for the large meal. The small meal serving is the same, but it is made with just one egg.

2 eggs

1 ounce (or 1 slice) of cheese, cut into pieces

1. In a small bowl, beat the eggs. Pour into a non-stick pan.
2. Place the cheese on top.
3. Put a lid on and cook at low heat, for about 5 minutes.

To your broccoli, you may add 1 tablespoon of light cheese spread. This has the same calories as 1 teaspoon of butter or margarine.

For dessert, enjoy 1 or 2 oatmeal cookies. Or in place of an oatmeal cookie, you could have a plain cookies such as a digestive or ginger snap.

Oatmeal Cookies

Makes 36 cookies.

1/3 cup margarine

3/4 cup packed brown sugar

1 egg

1/2 cup skim milk

1 teaspoon vanilla

1 cup flour

1 teaspoon baking powder

1 teaspoon baking soda

1 teaspoon cinnamon

1 1/2 cups rolled oats

1 cup raisins

1. In a large mixing bowl, mix together the margarine, brown sugar and egg. Beat with a wooden spoon until smooth. Beat in the milk and vanilla.
2. In a medium bowl, mix together the flour, baking powder, baking soda, cinnamon, and rolled oats.
3. Add the flour and oats to the large bowl. Stir well. Add the raisins and stir again.
4. Drop small spoonfuls of batter onto a non-stick baking sheet. Batter will be sticky. Bake in a 375°F oven for about ten minutes or until golden.

To keep your non-stick pans and non-stick cookie sheets in good shape, use a plastic spatula or plastic spoon rather than a metal one. Store your non-stick pans so that other pots aren't scratching them. I wrap mine in tea towels.

Your Dinner Menu	Large Meal	Small Meal
Cheese Omelet	1 large	1 small
Toast	2 slices	2 slices
Margarine	2 teaspoons	1 teaspoon
Broccoli	2 cups of pieces	2 cups of pieces
Light cheese spread	1 tablespoon	1 tablespoon
Oatmeal cookies	2	1

SMALL MEAL

DINNER 10

Ham & Sweet Potato

For this meal, buy a cooking ham. Look for one that has the least amount of fat. Put the ham on a rack in a roasting pan. Bake your ham for about twenty-five minutes per pound (1 1/2 hours per kg).

Hams have a small amount of either sugar or honey added. "Honey" ham does not have more sugar than regular ham.

Sweet potato can also be cooked by:
- *microwaving it at high for ten minutes*
- *boiling it with the skin on (take off the skin, once it is cooked).*

You can flavor and decorate the top of your ham by pushing about one dozen whole cloves into the outside of the ham. I usually put pineapple on top of the ham for the last half-hour of the cooking.

Mustard can be enjoyed with your ham.

A sweet potato (or yam) has different vitamins and minerals than a regular potato, and it's nice for a change. Since your oven is on, cook it like a regular baked potato. Poke it with a fork and cook until tender. Bake it for an hour.

Try these Seasoned Bread Crumbs sprinkled on your cauliflower.

You can make up some Seasoned Bread Crumbs to sprinkle on your cauliflower. You can sprinkle them on other vegetables and on baked dishes.

Seasoned Bread Crumbs

Makes just over 1 cup.

You can buy bread crumbs, or make your own by crushing dry bread and adding spices.

1 cup bread crumbs

2 tablespoons Parmesan cheese

1 tablespoon dried parsley

1 teaspoon oregano

1/2 teaspoon garlic powder

1/8 teaspoon pepper

Mix ingredients together. Store Seasoned Bread Crumbs in the fridge.

All vegetables are good choices but some, such as cauliflower, broccoli and yellow beans, have a higher amount of fiber and water. This makes them low in calories.

Low-calorie vegetables:

- asparagus
- green or yellow beans
- bean sprouts
- broccoli
- Brussels sprouts
- cabbage
- cauliflower
- celery
- cucumber
- eggplant
- fiddle heads
- leafy greens, such as lettuce and spinach
- marrow
- mushrooms
- okra
- onions
- green or red peppers
- radishes
- summer and spaghetti squash
- tomato
- zucchini

Whipped Gelatin

Makes 4 cups.

1 package light gelatin of your favorite flavor

1. Make the gelatin according to the directions on the box (or use the recipe on page 99).
2. Remove the gelatin from the fridge after about forty-five minutes. It should be as thick as an unbeaten egg white. Beat the gelatin with a beater until it is foamy and has doubled in size.
3. Put it back in the fridge until firm.

For dessert, have a dish of light gelatin. For variety, try whipping the gelatin. You can have twice as much when it is whipped.

Your Dinner Menu	Large Meal	Small Meal
Baked ham	1 thick slice (5 ounces, cooked)	1 thin slice (3 ounces, cooked)
Pineapple, packed in juice	3 rings, no juice	3 rings, no juice
Sweet potato	1 large	1 medium
Margarine	2 teaspoons	1 teaspoon
Cauliflower	2 cups	2 cups
Seasoned Bread Crumbs	1 teaspoon	1 teaspoon
Skim milk or 1 percent milk	1 cup	1 cup
Whipped Gelatin	1 cup	1 cup

SMALL MEAL

DINNER 11

Beef Stew

If you are in a hurry, try this:
Open a can of beef stew, put it in a pot and add some frozen or cooked vegetables. Cook until heated.

Beef stew served with potatoes and bread is an old favorite. This recipe is lower in fat, as it uses lean meat and only a small amount of added fat.

Vegetables that go well in a stew include turnips, yellow and green beans, carrots and peas. If you are in a rush, you can use frozen mixed vegetables in this recipe in place of the fresh vegetables.

Double the recipe if you want to make more to freeze for another day.

For dessert have a fruit serving.

Beef Stew

Recipe makes 7 cups.

1 tablespoon margarine or butter

2 medium onions, chopped

2 cloves garlic, chopped (or 1/2 teaspoon garlic powder)

1 pound stewing beef, remove any fat and chop (cut in the size of a "dice")

2 tablespoons flour

2 packets (or 2 cubes) beef bouillon mixed in 2 cups hot water

1 bay leaf (remove before serving)

2 large stalks of celery, sliced

3 medium carrots, sliced

2 cups other fresh vegetables (or frozen mixed vegetables)

1/8 teaspoon pepper

1/4 cup dry wine (or wine vinegar)

1. Place the margarine, onions and garlic in a heavy pot. Cook and stir on medium heat until the onions become clear. Stir often so they do not burn.
2. Add the meat and stir it until it is cooked on the outside (about five minutes). Sprinkle the flour over the onion and meat mixture, and stir until the flour disappears.
3. Take the pot off the heat while you add the rest of the ingredients. Stir. Return to heat. Bring to a boil and then turn the heat down to low. Cover and simmer for about an hour. Stir occasionally.
4. If you are using frozen mixed vegetables instead of fresh vegetables, add them just at the end and simmer for ten minutes.

North African Stew and Couscous

For a change, you may want a spicier stew. Try a North African beef stew. This stew would commonly be made with onions, carrots, turnips, tomatoes, zucchini, pumpkin and squash. When you cook the meat, add 1 teaspoon of each of the following: turmeric, cinnamon and cumin (or try 1 tablespoon of curry powder, instead), and 1 teaspoon of chili powder. Make this stew a day ahead so that the spice taste is best.

Instead of having this stew with bread and potatoes, you can serve it with couscous. Serve 1 1/4 cups couscous for the large meal and 1 cup for the small meal. Couscous is made from wheat and can be bought in all major food stores. It looks like rice and tastes like noodles. It is easy and quick to make because you just boil it in water. Serve the stew and couscous with mint tea.

Your Dinner Menu	Large Meal	Small Meal
Beef Stew	2 cups	1 1/2 cups
Boiled potatoes	1 large	1 medium
Bread	1 slice	1 slice
Margarine	1 teaspoon	1/2 teaspoon
Sliced cucumbers	1/2 medium cucumber	1/2 medium cucumber
Cantaloupe or melon	2 slices	2 slices

SMALL MEAL

DINNER 12

Fish & Chips

You could have store-bought chicken nuggets with your fries and vegetables instead of fish sticks.

- *for the large meal you could have 7 chicken nuggets (140 grams)*
- *for the small meal you could have 5 chicken nuggets (95 grams).*

Compare the calories of 10 french fries:

- *fried in oil from a restaurant – 160 calories.*
- *frozen fries baked in the oven – 90 calories.*
- *Baked Low-fat Fries – 60 calories.*

Bought packages of potato seasonings have sugar and salt. If you want to use these, use less than a tablespoon for this whole recipe.

This is an easy meal prepared with ready-made frozen fish sticks and frozen french fries. Bake them in the oven on a cookie sheet. The portions of fish sticks and the frozen french fries are kept small because of the fat in them. This meal has a lot less fat than battered fish and french fries that are deep-fried in oil.

Look for brands of fish sticks that are labeled low in fat. These are often made with less oil or a lighter batter.

You can also make Baked Low-Fat Fries at home using the recipe below. The photograph shows the store-bought frozen french fries, not these home-made ones.

Baked Low-Fat Fries

Makes 45 fries (15 fries for each potato)

3 small potatoes

1 egg white

1 teaspoon spices (choose from the spices listed on page 102 such as curry, dill or cajun spice)

1. Wash and peel the potatoes.
2. Cut into fry-size pieces or chunks.
3. In a small bowl, mix the egg white and spices with a fork.
4. Dip the potato pieces into the mixture.
5. Bake the potato pieces on a greased non-stick cookie sheet at 400°F. Cook for about thirty minutes, turning them every ten minutes.

With this meal, have one vegetable serving of squash, peas, carrots, corn, turnips or parsnips.

Here is how I cooked the squash shown in the photograph: cut a squash in half and place the cut side down on a cookie sheet. Bake in the oven with the fish and fries. Bake for half an hour, or until tender.

Try this light Jellied Vegetable Salad. It is colorful and tasty and low in calories. The lime gelatin gives it a nice green colour.

Jellied Vegetable Salad

Makes 2 1/2 cups (five servings).

1 package light lime gelatin

1 1/2 cups boiling water

2 tablespoons lemon or lime juice

1/2 cup finely chopped radish

1/2 cup finely chopped celery

1/2 cup finely chopped cabbage

1 tablespoon chopped fresh or dried parsley

1. In a medium bowl, place the gelatin powder. Add the boiling water and stir until the gelatin is mixed in. Add the lemon juice. Put this mixture in the fridge.
2. Chop all the vegetables. Once the mixture in the fridge is slightly thickened (about forty-five minutes), stir in all the vegetables.
3. Chill until set (about another hour).

Squash:
The orange squash shown in the photograph is an acorn squash. There are many kinds of squash. For example you may want to try spaghetti squash, one of the less sweet squashes.

***J**ellied Vegetable Salad can be a low-calorie vegetable choice with any lunch or dinner meal. A half cup has only 20 calories.*

***F**or a lightly salted and less sweet flavor in the Jellied Vegetable Salad, try this:*
- *add one packet of chicken bouillon mix, or one bouillon cube, to the boiling water.*

Your Dinner Menu	Large Meal	Small Meal
Fish sticks	6 sticks or 3 wedges	4 sticks or 2 wedges
Oven-baked frozen french fries	20	14
Ketchup	1 tablespoon	1 tablespoon
Squash	1/2 cup	1/2 cup
Jellied Vegetable Salad	1/2 cup	1/2 cup
Plum	1 medium	1 medium

SMALL MEAL

DINNER 13

Sausages & Corn Bread

Sausages are high in fat. However you choose to cook sausages, prick them with a fork several times so the fat can drain out of them. Here are some ways to cook them to remove some of the fat:

- broil in the oven on a rack inside a pan
- boil for ten minutes first, then finish by baking in the oven
- barbecue
- cook them in the microwave oven on a rack

Fill up on vegetables. Zucchini is a low-calorie vegetable that is easy to prepare by slicing and steaming. If you boil zucchini, it will get soggy.

Zucchini is also nice cooked in a pan with 1/2 teaspoon of margarine and chopped onion and garlic. To this you can add one or two other vegetables, such as:

- *canned or fresh chopped tomatoes*
- *green pepper*
- *eggplant*

Add water to the pan, if needed.

To add flavor to zucchini, sprinkle it after cooking with Parmesan cheese and pepper, or with Seasoned Bread Crumbs (see recipe on page 130).

Use the coleslaw recipe in Lunch 5 on page 80.

For a change, here are some starches that could take the place of two pieces of corn bread:

- 2 cups canned kernel corn or 2 small cobs of corn
- 1 1/4 cup rice

A 1/2 cup skim milk could replace the light ice cream bar.

Corn Bread

Makes an 8-inch square pan (twelve pieces).

3/4 cup cornmeal

1 1/4 cups skim milk

1 cup flour

1 tablespoon baking powder

1/2 teaspoon salt

1/4 cup sugar

1 egg, slightly beaten

3 level tablespoons shortening, butter or margarine, melted

1. In a medium bowl, mix together the cornmeal and milk. Set aside for five minutes.
2. In a large bowl, mix together the flour, baking powder, salt and sugar.
3. In a small bowl, mix the slightly beaten egg and the melted fat. Add this to the cornmeal mixture.
4. Add the liquid mixture to the flour mixture. Stir only until combined. The batter will be lumpy. Pour into an 8-inch square pan. Use a non-stick pan, or grease your pan lightly.
5. Bake in a 400°F oven for about twenty minutes, or until lightly browned.
6. Cut into twelve pieces (about 3-inches by 2-inches).

Your Dinner Menu	Large Meal	Small Meal
Sausages	4 small links	3 small links
Corn Bread	2 1/2 pieces	2 pieces
Margarine	2 teaspoons	–
Steamed zucchini	2 cups	2 cups
Seasoned Bread Crumbs	1 tablespoon	1 tablespoon
Coleslaw	1/2 cup	1/2 cup
Light fudge ice cream bar	1 bar	1 bar

Small Meal

DINNER 14

Chili Con Carne

Chili freezes well. You can easily double the recipe for freezing.

Chili Con Carne

Makes 6 1/4 cups.

1 pound lean ground beef

2 medium onions, chopped

28 ounce (796 ml) can kidney beans

10 ounce (284 ml) can tomato soup

1/8 teaspoon pepper

1/2 teaspoon chili powder

1 tablespoon vinegar

1/2 teaspoon Worcestershire sauce

1 cup chopped vegetables, such as celery or green pepper

See page 102 for more about rice and how to cook it.

Instead of 1/2 cup of rice:

- *1 1/2 slices of bread*
- *half a piece of bannock*
- *1 small potato*

1. In a large, heavy pot, brown the ground beef. Drain off as much fat as you can.
2. Add all the other ingredients to the pot.
3. Cover with a lid and cook for two to three hours on low heat. Stir every now and then so the chili doesn't stick. Add extra water if it gets too thick.

Serve the meal with brown or white rice.

Add a low-calorie vegetable such as yellow beans or green beans. Carrot sticks are served on the side.

For a dessert treat, try this tasty Baked Apple recipe or have a serving of any other kind of fruit.

Baked Apple

Makes two baked apples.

2 medium apples

1 teaspoon butter or margarine

1 tablespoon brown sugar

1/4 teaspoon cinnamon

1/4 teaspoon lemon juice

Dash of nutmeg (if desired)

1 tablespoon raisins

1. Remove apple core, cutting from the top of the apple. Don't cut right through to the bottom. Prick apples with a fork.
2. In a small bowl, mix together the other ingredients and spoon into the apples.
3. Place apples on a dish and microwave them on high for one minute and twenty seconds, or until the apples are tender. Or place the apples in a pan with 2 tablespoons of water and bake in a 350°F oven for thirty minutes.

A baked apple helps satisfy a sweet tooth, and has less fat and sugar than a piece of apple pie.

- *A 3 1/2-inch piece of apple pie usually has about 7 teaspoons of added sugar and starch and 3 teaspoons of added fat.*
- *One of these Baked Apples has 1 1/2 teaspoons of added sugar and 1/2 teaspoon of added fat.*

These baked apples have a lovely glaze because of the combination of brown sugar and butter. Margarine can be used instead, but butter makes the syrup thicker.

This recipe has less fat and sugar than a traditional baked apple. Regular sugar is used because low-calorie sweeteners tend to make the syrup in the apple too thin.

Your Dinner Menu	Large Meal	Small Meal
Chili Con Carne	1 1/2 cups	1 cup
Rice	1/2 cup	1/3 cup
Green beans	1 cup	1 cup
Carrot sticks	1 medium carrot	1 medium carrot
Baked Apple	1	1

Small Meal

DINNER 15

Perogies

P*erogies and sour cream go together like hugs and kisses; but go for a light hug. Enjoy 1 tablespoon of light sour cream, or 2 tablespoons of fat-free sour cream with your perogies.*

- *Fat-free sour cream has only 9 calories in a tablespoon.*
- *Light sour cream (7% fat) has 16 calories in 1 tablespoon.*
- *Regular sour cream (14% fat) has 32 calories in 1 tablespoon.*

Buy frozen perogies and enjoy a fast-food meal, at home. Perogies come with many fillings, such as cheese, potato, cottage cheese and even pizza.

First, fry onions at low heat in 1 teaspoon of fat. Then take the onions out of the pan so they don't get overcooked. Fry the perogies in the same pan until lightly browned. Another way to cook them is to boil them for ten minutes.

Instead of having a 2-ounce piece of garlic sausage (kolbasa) with the large meal, you could have:

- 1 cup of 1 percent cottage cheese
- 2 slices bologna, broiled or fried, without added fat

Instead of the beet soup, you may want to have 1 cup of cooked beets. Pickled beets have added sugar, so 1/2 cup of these would equal 1 cup of beet soup.

Easy Beet Soup

Makes 3 1/2 cups.

10 ounce (398 ml) can diced beets (unsweetened)
1 1/2 cups vegetable juice (such as V-8 juice)
2 cups chopped cabbage
1/4 teaspoon dried dill weed

1. Place all ingredients in a pot.
2. Cover and simmer. Stir as it is cooking. It will take about fifteen minutes to cook.

Serve with a dab of low-fat sour cream and green onion tops.

For a low-calorie vegetable, have sauerkraut or a dill pickle. A low-salt alternative to sauerkraut or a pickle would be a small salad.

For dessert have one fresh peach. If you want canned peaches, have two halves with 2 tablespoons of juice. Choose fruit canned in water or juice. Have one plain cookie with your fruit. Plain bought cookies include arrowroot biscuits, digestives, raisin cookies (as shown in the photograph), ginger snaps, oatmeal cookies and Graham wafers.

Your Dinner Menu	Large Meal	Small Meal
Perogies	6	4
Low-fat or fat-free sour cream	1 tablespoon	1 tablespoon
Cooked sliced onion	1/2 small onion	1/2 small onion
in margarine	1 teaspoon	1 teaspoon
Garlic sausage	2 ounces	1 ounce
Easy Beet Soup	1 cup	1 cup
Cherry tomatoes	2, or 2 slices of tomato	2, or 2 slices of tomato
Sauerkraut	1/2 cup	1/2 cup
Peach	1	1
Plain cookie	1	1

Small Meal

DINNER 16

Hamburger with Potato Salad

Hamburger safety:
Cook hamburgers until well done to make sure they are safe to eat. There must be no pink showing. Refrigerate any leftovers right away.

Use lean or extra-lean ground hamburger when you make hamburgers. One pound of lean hamburger will make three large or four medium cooked hamburger patties. For extra flavor you can mix spices or two teaspoons of dried onion soup into the raw hamburger.

Here are several ways to cook your hamburgers:
- grill on a barbecue
- place them on a rack and broil in the oven
- fry them in a non-stick pan, and soak up the extra fat with a paper towel

Fill your hamburger bun with lots of lettuce, tomato and onion. Add a teaspoon of ketchup, mustard, and relish or cheese spread, if you wish. For the large meal, add one slice of cheese.

If you would like to have hot dogs (wiener in a bun with onion, ketchup and mustard) instead of hamburgers, you can have:
- instead of the cheeseburger for the large meal, two hot dogs with no cheese.
- instead of a hamburger for the small meal, one hot dog with cheese.

Check the label of light iced tea packages:
- *Make sure the tea you buy has fewer than 20 calories in a serving.*
- *It will probably say "diet", "calorie-reduced" or "light ("lite") on the label.*

A nice drink for this meal is light iced tea. There are many kinds that you can buy. You could make your own light iced tea by mixing leftover cold tea with lemon juice and a low-calorie sweetener, to suit your taste.

Watermelon or some other fresh fruit is a great end to this meal.

This light potato salad goes nicely with your hamburger.

Potato Salad

Makes 4 cups of potato salad.

4 small cooked potatoes, chopped

1/2 green pepper, finely chopped

2 celery stalks, finely chopped

2 to 3 green onions, finely chopped (or 1 small onion)

5 radishes, sliced

2 tablespoons vinegar

2 tablespoons light mayonnaise

1/2 teaspoon prepared mustard

Salt and pepper, to taste

1 hard boiled egg, chopped

Dash of paprika to sprinkle on top

1. In a big bowl, mix together the potatoes, green pepper, celery, green onions and radishes.
2. In a small bowl, mix together the vinegar, mayonnaise, mustard, salt and pepper. Gently fold in the chopped egg. Pour this into the bowl with the potatoes, and mix gently. Sprinkle the top with paprika.
3. Refrigerate until ready to eat.

Potato salad safety: *Refrigerate leftover potato salad as soon as your meal is over.*

Your Dinner Menu	**Large Meal**	**Small Meal**
Cheeseburger / Hamburger with bun and toppings	large burger, with cheese	medium burger
Potato Salad	3/4 cup	1/2 cup
Celery sticks	2 stalks	2 stalks
Dill pickles	2 small, or 1 medium	2 small, or 1 medium
Light iced tea	12 ounces	12 ounces
Watermelon	3 small slices	3 small slices

SMALL MEAL

DINNER 17

Roast Turkey Dinner

Roast turkey is a great meal to have any time of the year. The leftovers come in so handy for sandwiches and other meals. I've made this meal fancier by adding some extras. Even with the extras, the calories in this meal are not any higher than the other meals.

I leave my turkey unstuffed. Bread stuffing is made with a lot of fat and soaks up more fat from the turkey.

Turkey

- Place your turkey on a rack, breast side up in an uncovered pan. Cover with lid or tin foil if drying out.
- Cook your turkey for about fifteen minutes per pound in a 350°F oven.
- Once cooked, remove the high-fat skin, and slice the dark and white meat. Dark meat has more fat than white meat.
- Enjoy 1 tablespoon of canned or home-made cranberry sauce on the side.

If you decide to have regular gravy, limit yourself to 1 tablespoon.

Potatoes and Gravy

- Use the recipe for Low-Fat Gravy (page 106) and Low-Fat Mashed Potatoes (page 122).

Vegetables

- A lot of vegetables are served with this meal, including carrots, peas, dill pickles, Jellied Vegetable Salad (see recipe on page 139) and asparagus (fresh or canned).

If you would prefer to not have alcohol:
- *use non-alcohol wine in the spritzer*
- *drink diet soft drink, sparkling mineral water or soda water*

Beverage

In addition to your glass of water, this meal is served with a wine spritzer. A spritzer has fewer calories and alcohol than regular wine. To make a glass of spritzer, add to a glass 2 ounces (1/4 cup) of dry wine, and fill up the glass with diet ginger ale or diet 7-up.

Dessert

This crustless pumpkin pie is delicious. When I served this to my family, they didn't even miss the crust. It can be served as it is, or with 1-2 tablespoons of a frozen whipped topping.

Crustless Pumpkin Pie

Makes six slices (9-inch deep pie plate).

14 ounce (398 ml) can pumpkin
1/2 cup sugar
1/2 teaspoon salt
1/2 teaspoon ginger
1 teaspoon cinnamon
1/4 teaspoon nutmeg
1/4 teaspoon cloves
2 slightly beaten eggs
13 ounce (385 ml) can evaporated skim milk

1. In a large bowl, mix pumpkin, sugar, salt and spices.
2. Stir in the two slightly beaten eggs until well mixed.
3. Add the evaporated skim milk (shake can before opening) and stir until smooth.
4. Pour into a lightly greased pie plate and bake in 400°F oven for about forty minutes, or until knife inserted near the center of the pie comes out clean.

Other options for a topping would include whipping cream in a squirt can, packaged mixed toppings or vanilla yogurt. Check the label; whipped topping should have fewer than 20 calories in a 2-tablespoon serving.

I think this pie is best if made the day before.

Your Dinner Menu	Large Meal	Small Meal
Turkey	3 ounces white meat and 2 ounces of dark meat	3 ounces white meat (or 2 ounces white and 1 ounce dark)
Cranberry sauce	2 teaspoons	2 teaspoons
Low-Fat Mashed Potatoes	1 1/4 cups	3/4 cups
Low-Fat Gravy	4 tablespoons	2 tablespoons
Peas and carrots	1/2 cup	1/2 cup
Asparagus	7 stalks	7 stalks
Dill pickle	1 medium	1 medium
Jellied Vegetable Salad	1/2 cup	1/2 cup
Wine spritzer	1/2 cup	1/2 cup
Crustless Pumpkin Pie	1 slice	1 slice
Whipped topping	2 tablespoons (not all shown in photo)	2 tablespoons (not all shown in photo)

SMALL MEAL

DINNER 18

Baked Macaroni & Cheese

Instead of two eggs, use a small tin of water-packed tuna with the water drained.

Use a low-fat cheese in this recipe and you will be eating less fat.

For extra flavor, add one of these to macaroni and cheese:
- *dash of hot chili sauce*
- *1 tablespoon of salsa*
- *1/4 teaspoon of both oregano and garlic powder*

Baked Macaroni and Cheese

Makes about 5 1/2 cups.

2 cups dry macaroni

2 tablespoons skim milk

2 eggs, beaten with a fork

1/2 a can (5 ounces or 142 ml) tomato soup

1/2 cup loosely packed, shredded Cheddar cheese

2 tablespoons Seasoned Bread Crumbs (see page 131), if baked

1. Fill a heavy pot with water and bring to a boil. Add the macaroni and boil for ten minutes. Drain.
2. Add the milk, then the eggs, to the macaroni and stir quickly on low heat until the eggs are cooked. Add the tomato soup and cheese and stir some more. It should be ready in two minutes.
3. It is ready to eat now if you want. If you want it baked (as in the picture), place it in a baking dish and sprinkle Seasoned Bread Crumbs on top. Bake in a 375°F oven for half an hour.

Vegetables
- Cut broccoli in pieces and steam or lightly boil. For other low-calorie vegetable choices see page 131.
- Try raw pieces of rutabaga or turnip. For a change, cook turnip with carrots, and mash together once cooked.

For dessert, try this easy and delicious dessert, made with bananas, pineapple, pudding and Graham wafers. It looks as good as it tastes.

Pineapple Surprise

Makes six servings.

1 1/2 cups skim milk

1 package light banana instant pudding mix

1 cup frozen whipped topping (regular or light), thawed

8 ounces (xxx ml) can crushed pineapple, drained

2 small bananas, sliced thinly

1/4 cup Graham cracker crumbs (equal to about 4 Graham crackers)

You may want to make Pineapple Surprise with regular pudding instead of light. By doing so, you will add an extra 2 1/2 teaspoons of sugar to each serving.

1. Pour the skim milk into a medium bowl and add the pudding mix.
2. Beat with a whisk or an electric mixer until thickened (about two minutes).
3. Fold in the frozen whipped topping and pineapple until well blended.
4. Add the sliced bananas and Graham cracker crumbs to the pudding mixture. Save some bananas and crumbs for the top. If you want, you can layer the pudding mixture, bananas and crumbs.
5. Put in the fridge until ready to serve.

Your Dinner Menu	Large Meal	Small Meal
Baked Macaroni & Cheese	2 cups	1 1/4 cups
Broccoli	1 1/2 cups	1 1/2 cups
Rutabaga or turnip sticks	1/2 cup	1/2 cup
Bread & butter pickles	5 slices	5 slices
Pineapple Surprise	1 serving	1 serving

SMALL MEAL

DINNER 19

Pork Chop & Applesauce

You can place a rack over a pan and broil the meat in the oven. The fat falls into the pan.

Here are some lower fat cuts of pork:
- *loin or tenderloin*
- *leg, inside round*

Pork does not have to be a rich meal. Trim the fat and barbecue or broil small pork chops. Or cook without fat in a non-stick pan. Pork goes nicely with boiled potatoes sprinkled with fresh or dried parsley.

A small dish of applesauce is served with the pork chop. Instead of applesauce, you could slice an apple and an onion and cook them with the pork.

For another nice change, try a lamb chop with mint sauce, instead of pork chop with applesauce.

This meal is served with an easy-to-make German Bean Salad. This salad will keep in the fridge for a week. Try making it with a flavored vinegar, as shown in the picture at the side.

German Bean Salad

Makes 4 cups

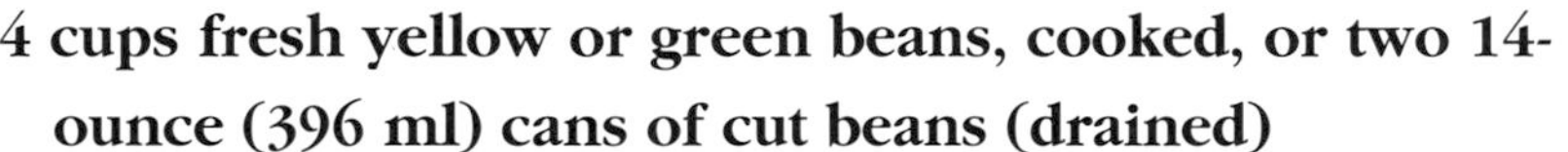

4 cups fresh yellow or green beans, cooked, or two 14-ounce (396 ml) cans of cut beans (drained)

1/2 medium onion, thinly sliced

2 tablespoon vinegar

1/4 teaspoon salt (no salt if using canned beans)

1. Cut the beans into 1-inch pieces and place in a salad bowl. If you are using canned beans, drain them and place them in the bowl.
2. Mix with the other ingredients.
3. Leave to stand for thirty minutes. Serve.

Tapioca pudding is easy to make and healthy. Instead of this pudding you may choose a boxed light pudding, or one of the dessert choices from the other meals, or one cup of milk with a plain cookie.

Tapioca Pudding

Makes four servings.

1 egg (separated)

2 tablespoons sugar

2 cups skim milk

3 tablcspoons quick-cooking tapioca

3 tablespoons sugar

Dash of salt

1/2 teaspoon vanilla

1. Place the egg white in a bowl and the egg yolk in a small pan. Beat the egg white with a beater until foamy. Gradually add 2 tablespoons of sugar until mixture forms soft peaks.
2. In the pan, beat the yolk with a fork. Add the milk to the yolk. Stir in tapioca, then add 3 tablespoons of sugar and salt.
3. Cook this yolk mixture to a rolling boil, stirring. Take off heat.
4. Pour a small amount of the tapioca mixture over the beaten egg white and blend. Fold the rest of the tapioca mixture into the egg white. Cool on the counter.
5. Stir tapioca after fifteen minutes. Add vanilla and chill.
6. Before serving, put 1 teaspoon of diet jam or a small piece of fruit on top of each serving, if you want.

Your Dinner Menu	Large Meal	Small Meal
Pork chop	1 medium (5 ounces, cooked)	1 small (3 ounces, cooked)
Applesauce	1/4 cup	1/4 cup
Boiled potatoes with parsley	8 small or 1 large	5 small or 1 large
German Bean Salad	1 cup	1 cup
Tapioca Pudding	1 serving	1 serving
Coffee	1 cup	1 cup

SMALL MEAL

DINNER 20

Tacos

You can make tacos with a lot or a little spice. You can make tacos using the bean and meat filling below, or using leftover spaghetti sauce, chili con carne or chopped turkey or meat. Tacos are a favorite with my family. Tacos are so easy and my kids love to help (even if it does get a bit messy making them; and eating them). For a change, you can make burritos by using a soft flour tortilla shell instead of a hard taco shell.

You could make tacos one day and burritos the next with the rest of the Bean and Meat Filling. If you're cooking for just one or two people, you'll have some extra to freeze.

Canned refried beans have a lot of fat and are not a good choice.

Here are some low-calorie vegetables that taste good in tacos:
- *bean sprouts*
- *chopped tomatoes*
- *chopped green peppers*
- *shredded lettuce*
- *salsa*

Bean and Meat Filling

Makes 5 cups (enough for twenty tacos).

1 pound lean hamburger

1/3 cup water

1 package taco or burrito spice mix

28 ounce (796 ml) can kidney beans or white beans, including the juice

1. In a medium pot, brown the hamburger. Drain off as much fat as you can.
2. Stir in the water and spice mix. Cook on medium heat for ten minutes. Add extra water if needed. Add the beans and cook for another five minutes.

Tacos

To make each taco you will need:

1 taco shell

1/4 cup Bean and Meat Filling

1 tablespoon shredded cheese

Lots of vegetables

1. Heat the taco shells in the oven at 350° for 5 minutes.
2. Into each hot taco shell put the meat and bean mixture, cheese and vegetables.

Since you eat burritos or tacos with your hands, it's nice to serve other finger foods, too. Try fresh vegetables with this dip.

Vegetable Dip

Makes 1 1/2 cups.

1 cup plain skim milk yogurt

1/2 cup low-fat sour cream

2 tablespoons dried onion soup mix

Chopped green onion tops or parsley

1. Mix the first three ingredients together.
2. Put the green onions or parsley on top.

For dessert, make an angel food cake from a mix, or even easier, buy one from a bakery. Angel food cake has the lowest amount of fat of any cake. Serve the angel food cake with fruit, such as strawberries (either fresh or unsweetened frozen), and a dab of frozen or canned whipped topping. Other topping choices are listed on page 159.

Your Dinner Menu	Large Meal	Small Meal
Bean & Meat Tacos	3	2
Fresh vegetables on the side	2 cups	2 cups
Vegetable Dip	2 tablespoons	2 tablespoons
Angel food cake	3-inch slice	3-inch slice
Strawberries	1/2 cup	1/2 cup
Whipped topping	1 tablespoon	1 tablespoon

SMALL MEAL

DINNER 21

Liver & Onions

Calf liver is the tastiest and most tender, but it costs more than beef liver. Chicken liver is cheap, tender and tasty. Pork liver is a bit stronger tasting than beef liver.

You can cook beef kidney as a change from beef liver.

Boil chicken gizzards in a bit of chicken broth for at least an hour until they are tender.

Iron is needed for healthy blood. Organ meats are one of the best sources of iron. Other good sources include beef, pork and chicken, eggs, oysters, kidney beans, whole-wheat bread, cereals, spinach, dark green lettuce and dried fruit such as raisins.

Do you love liver? Then you'll enjoy this meal. Organ meats such as liver, kidney, gizzards and heart are all rich in iron. But they are also high in cholesterol, so eat small servings, as shown.

Liver and Onions

Makes enough for 3 medium or 4 large servings.

1 medium onion, thinly sliced

1/2 cup beef broth made from 1/2 cup water plus 1 packet (or 1 cube) beef bouillon mix

1/4 cup dry wine or wine vinegar

1 pound (454 grams) beef liver

1. Heat up the beef broth and wine in a non-stick or cast-iron pan. Over low heat, cook the onion slices until soft. Take the onions out of the pan, leaving the liquid.
2. Place the liver in the pan and cook it on high heat for a few minutes on each side. Make sure it is cooked through but not overcooked. Overcooking makes liver tough. Just before serving, return the onions to the pan to warm them up.
3. At the table, pour the broth from the pan over your liver and rice, if desired.

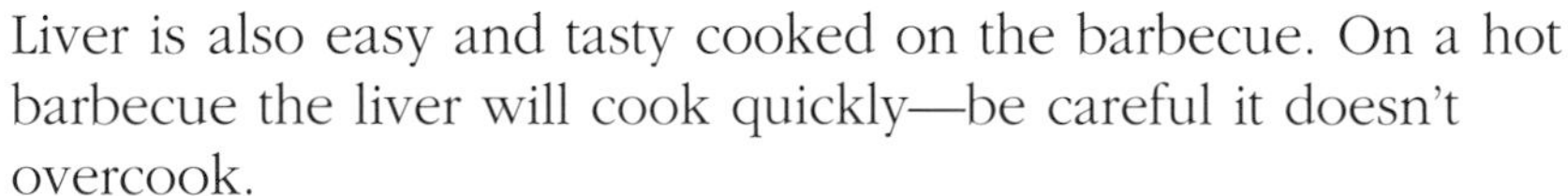

Liver is also easy and tasty cooked on the barbecue. On a hot barbecue the liver will cook quickly—be careful it doesn't overcook.

For your starch, you may have rice, as shown, or potatoes.

The vegetables for this meal are carrots and tomatoes. Choose either canned tomatoes or fresh sliced tomatoes.

For dessert there is fruit salad served with two small vanilla wafers (or one plain cookie, such as an Arrowroot biscuit). To make your fruit salad, mix together any of your favorite fresh or frozen fruits.

Your Dinner Menu	Large Meal	Small Meal
Liver	2 slices (large serving)	1 slice (medium serving)
Cooked sliced onions	1/2 cup	1/2 cup
Rice	1 cup	3/4 cup
Carrots	1/2 cup	1/2 cup
Canned tomatoes	1 cup	1 cup
Fresh fruit salad	1 cup	1 cup
Vanilla wafers	2 small	2 small

SMALL MEAL

DINNER 22

Sun Burger

These meatless burgers are delicious when served on a bagel or hamburger bun. Add to your bagel: lots of vegetables, such as lettuce, tomatoes, onions and cucumbers.

Sun Burgers

Makes 12 burgers.

1 1/2 cups cooked rice, brown or white

19 ounce (540 ml) can romano beans (or other beans, such as pinto or kidney)

1/3 cup sesame seeds

1/3 cup sunflower seeds

2 tablespoons wheat germ

1/4 teaspoon basil

1/4 teaspoon pepper

1/2 teaspoon garlic powder

1 teaspoon parsley flakes

1 teaspoon of dried dill weed

1 egg

1 cup loosely packed, shredded mozzarella cheese

Using a low-fat cheese will reduce the fat.

1. Cook rice or use cold rice from the night before.
2. Drain the beans. Put them in a small bowl and mash them with a fork or a masher.
3. In a large bowl, mix all the ingredients. Mix with a large spoon or fork, or use your hands.
4. Form mixture into patties. Cook until nicely browned in a non-stick frying pan or heavy frying pan (lightly greased).

Kale and Orange Salad

This salad is made with kale leaves, and slices of bok choy, broccoli, oranges and strawberries. Remove the tough stem of the kale and chop the leaves in fine strips. Use your favorite salad dressing, and try a sprinkle of sesame seeds on top.

The salad with this meal is rich in calcium, iron and vitamin C.

This dessert is easy to make and has a nice light flavor.

Dream Delight

Makes four 1-cup servings.

1 package light gelatin, raspberry or any other flavor
1 package unflavored gelatin
1 package dessert topping mix (enough to make 2 cups)
1 1/4 cups boiling water
1 1/4 cups cold water

1. Place the light gelatin and the unflavored gelatin in a bowl.
2. Add 1 1/4 cups boiling water. Stir until the gelatin is mixed in. Then add 1 1/4 cups cold water and stir. Refrigerate.
3. Remove the gelatin from the fridge after about forty-five minutes. It should be as thick as an unbeaten egg white. Do not allow the gelatin to get too firm.
4. Mix the dry whipped topping mix as shown on the box.
5. Blend topping with a beater into gelatin mixture until well mixed.
6. Pour into four dessert bowls. Refrigerate to set.

You may want to make this dessert with regular gelatin instead of light. By doing so, you will add an extra 4 teaspoons of sugar to each serving.

Your Dinner Menu	Large Meal	Small Meal
Sun Burgers	2	1
Bagel	1	1
Light mayonnaise	2 teaspoons	1/2 teaspoon
Kale and Orange Salad	large	large
Oil-free salad dressing	1 tablespoon	1 tablespoon
Dream Delight	1 cup	1 cup

SMALL MEAL

DINNER 23 Salmon & Potato Dish

Add one of these to your salmon for some extra flavor:
- *1/2 teaspoon horseradish*
- *1/4 teaspoon mustard*
- *1 tablespoon salsa*
- *1 tablespoon spaghetti sauce*

- *Seasoned Bread Crumbs (page 130) or Parmesan cheese can be sprinkled on top of this dish.*
- *Instant mashed potatoes can be used. They are softer and moister than fresh mashed potatoes.*

This is one of the meals that my husband likes to make. It is easy and is always popular. It can be made with canned salmon or tuna, or any kind of leftover fish.

Salmon and Potato Dish

Makes one small baking dish (2 large or 3 small servings).

1 can (213 g) of pink salmon (canned in water)
Dash of pepper
2 cups mashed potato (leftover or fresh)
1 cup loosely packed, shredded Cheddar cheese

1. Drain the water from the salmon can. Mash the salmon with bones. Put the salmon on the bottom of a small baking dish. Sprinkle with pepper and half the shredded cheese.
2. On top of the salmon and cheese spread the mashed potato.
3. Sprinkle the rest of the cheese on top.
4. Bake in a 350°F oven for half an hour, or microwave for eight minutes.

For a change, this dish can also be made into patties and fried in a non-stick pan.

Corn is the sweet vegetable with this meal, and spinach and tomato juice are the low-calorie vegetables.

Spinach is rich in iron.

You can buy spinach fresh or frozen.

Choose either 1/3 cup of creamed corn or 1/2 cup of kernel corn for your vegetable. Creamed corn has sugar added, so a smaller serving is enough.

The dessert is light gelatin with fruit.

Light Gelatin with Fruit

Makes three 1-cup servings.

1 package light gelatin

1 cup boiling water

1/4 cup cold water

14-ounce (398 ml) can fruit cocktail, with juice

1. Put the gelatin in a medium bowl (not plastic).
2. Add the boiling water. Stir until gelatin is all mixed in.
3. Add the cold water and fruit cocktail and stir.
4. Pour into three dessert bowls. Regrigerate to set.

Instead of fruit cocktail, you can use a can of other fruit such as peaches. Chop the fruit into pieces.

If you want, you can use 1 3/4 cups of fresh chopped fruit instead of canned fruit. When you use fresh fruit, add 1 cup of cold water instead of 1/4 cup.

Your Dinner Menu	Large Meal	Small Meal
Salmon & Potato Dish	1/2 the recipe	1/3 the recipe
Corn	3/4 cup	1/2 cup
Spinach	1/2 cup	1/2 cup
Tomato juice	1/2 cup	1/2 cup
Celery	1/4 stalk (in tomato juice)	1 1/4 stalk
Light Gelatin with Fruit	1 cup	1 cup

SMALL MEAL

DINNER 24

Hamburger Noodle Dish

Most packages of noodles and sauce mix that can be added to help hamburger are high in fat. This recipe is lower in fat.

Hamburger Noodle Dish

Makes 7 1/3 cups (about 4 large or 6 small servings).

1 pound lean hamburger

1 large onion, chopped

1/4 teaspoon pepper

10 ounce (284 ml) can tomato soup

10 ounce (284 ml) can mushroom pieces (drained)

1 cup skim milk

1 teaspoon Worcestershire sauce

4 cups dry corkscrew noodles (or 2 1/2 cups macaroni)

1. In a large heavy pan, brown the hamburger. Drain off all the fat.
2. Add the chopped onion to the hamburger and cook until the onions are soft. Add water if too dry. Add all other ingredients except the noodles. Cook for fifteen minutes.
3. While the hamburger and onions are cooking, add the noodles to a pot of boiling water. Drain the cooked noodles.
4. Add cooked noodles to the hamburger mixture. Cook for five more minutes.

The mushrooms add a nice flavor to this recipe.

If you want a bit more zip, you can always add a dash of hot pepper sauce.

The corkscrew noodles look nice in this dish, but if you don't have them, use macaroni.

This meal is served with mixed vegetables and steamed cabbage. You may drizzle 1 tablespoon of light cheese spread on your cabbage, instead of the butter or margarine.

For dessert, have a piece of fresh fruit.

Your Dinner Menu	Large Meal	Small Meal
Hamburger Noodle Dish	1 3/4 cups	1 1/4 cups
Mixed vegetables	1 cup	3/4 cup
Cabbage	1 cup	1 cup
Margarine or butter	1 teaspoon	1/2 teaspoon
Grapes	1 1/4 cups (33 grapes)	1 1/4 cups (33 grapes)

SMALL MEAL

DINNER 25

Pizza

This meal can be eaten out in a restaurant or you can make the meal at home using the recipe below. The photograph shows a thick crust pizza. You may want to choose a thin crust pizza which will have less calories. Choose a pizza with lots of vegetables and don't go heavy on the meat and cheese.

If you are making your own pizza at home, you can make it lower in fat by using lean meat and low-fat cheese, and lots of vegetables of your choice. Try this easy recipe.

Pizza Sauce:
Mix one 14 ounce (398 ml) can of tomato sauce with 1/2 teaspoon oregano and 1/2 teaspoon garlic powder.

For extra flavor, add in:
- *1 small onion (finely chopped)*
- *1 clove chopped garlic (instead of powder)*
- *1/2 stalk chopped celery*
- *pinch of cinnamon and cloves*

Homemade Pizza

Makes one 12-inch pizza (8 medium slices).

Pizza shell (ready-made, 12-inch)

1 cup Pizza Sauce (see sidebar)

Vegetables, such as mushrooms, peppers, onions, tomatoes, broccoli, zucchini, or eggplant

1/2 cup pineapple chunks

2 ounces of sliced ham, sausage or pepperoni

3/4 cup loosely packed low-fat shredded cheese

1. Spread the pizza sauce on the pizza shell.
2. Add the vegetables, pineapple and meat. Top with cheese.
3. Place on your oven rack or use a pizza pan, if you have one. Bake in a 350°F oven for fifteen minutes, until the cheese bubbles.

You can also make mini pizzas on opened hamburger buns.

Have a salad with your pizza. With your meal enjoy a diet soft drink (as shown) or a small glass of tomato juice. Also have water to drink.

Have a fruit for dessert.

A few restaurant tips:

- Start with a salad, clear soup or vegetable soup. Even fast food restaurants now have salads.
- Ask for low-fat salad dressings on the side.
- Eat a fruit or a fresh vegetable snack before you go to a restaurant so you won't be so hungry and overeat.
- It may help if you decide what you'll order before you go. Or better still, decide what you won't order.
- Don't be shy about asking for foods to be made to your liking. For example, if you order a sandwich, ask for it to be unbuttered.
- If your meal is bigger than your portions should be, ask the waiter to package your leftovers, so you can take them home.

Your Dinner Menu	Large Meal	Small Meal
12-inch Pizza	2 medium slices	1 large slice
Salad	large	large
Oil-free salad dressing	1 tablespoon	1 tablespoon
Diet soft drink	large	large
Nectarine	1	1

SMALL MEAL

DINNER 26

Grilled Chicken Bun & Fries

Yes, you may still eat out at fast food restaurants—occasionally. Most foods in restaurants are high in fat.

Since fries are the most common food ordered in restaurants, they are included in this meal; but choose a small order.

If you decide to make this meal at home, make Baked Low-Fat Fries (page 138), baked frozen french fries or a baked potato.

Instead of a grilled chicken breast on a bun (as shown in the photograph), you could order:

- a small serving of six chicken nuggets with sauce
- a single fish burger
- a cheeseburger

Salad with a light dressing is included with this meal. No salad dressing is included with the small meal due to the calories (see side bar). In a restaurant, the best choice is to have your salad plain or with half a package of "light" vinegar-based dressing (vinaigrette).

Since this meal is higher in fat than other meals, a dessert is not included with the small meal.

Have water and a diet soft drink, if you like.

Try to enjoy your coffee or tea with no milk or sugar, or less of both.

Salad dressings:

- *Some of the "light" salad dressings in restaurants are still high in calories. They can have up to 60 calories in one package. Check the label*
- *The regular salad dressings in restaurants may have 200 calories in one package.*

Your Dinner Menu	**Large Meal**	**Small Meal**
Grilled chicken on a bun	1	1
French fries	1 small order	1 small order
Ketchup	1 tablespoon	1 tablespoon
Salad	1 small	1 small (optional)
Light vinaigrette salad dressing	1 package	–
Diet soft drink	large	large
Yogurt cone	1 small	–

FAMILY
OF
FINE CARS
SMALL MEAL

DINNER 27

Chinese Stir Fry

Put your rice on to cook before you start making the stir-fry.

Other protein choices
Instead of raw meat, chicken, or fish, you could use:
- *5 ounces of leftover cooked chicken, meat or fish*
- *7 ounces of shrimp (23 jumbo shrimp)*
- *1/2 cup firm tofu (cut in chunks)*
- *28 almonds.*

Wash your knife and cutting board with hot soapy water if you use raw chicken or raw meat.

If you are making Chinese food at home, use little or no fat in a pot, or a non-stick pan or wok. Your pan has to be large enough to hold all the vegetables.

Chinese Stir Fry

Makes 4 cups (2 large meal servings).

3/4 cup (or 6 ounces) raw lean red meat, chicken or fish (thinly sliced)*

1 packet chicken or beef bouillon mix

2 tablespoons water

1 small onion

1 to 2 cloves chopped garlic

4 to 6 cups loosely packed vegetable pieces

2 teaspoons cornstarch

1/4 cup cold water

1 tablespoon soy sauce

1/4 teaspoon ginger powder

1. Chop up or slice your onion, garlic and 4 cups of vegetables. I usually put in one bowl the vegetables that need the most cooking, such as carrots and broccoli. In a second bowl I put the vegetables that need less cooking, such as bean sprouts. Put the bowls of vegetables to the side.
2. Place the raw meat (or other protein choice) in your cold wok or frying pan. Sprinkle the bouillon mix on your meat and stir. Add 2 tablespoons of water. Heat up your wok or frying pan and cook for about three minutes. If you are using cooked leftover meat instead of raw meat, it doesn't need to be cooked first.
3. Add the onions, garlic and first bowl of vegetables. Stir at high heat for five to ten minutes until cooked. Now add the second bowl of vegetables.
4. In a small bowl, mix together the cornstarch, 1/4 cup of cold water, soy sauce and ginger. Add this to your wok. Cook for another minute or two.

Fresh vegetables are best in a stir-fry, but you could also use frozen or canned vegetables. Try any of these vegetables:

- bamboo shoots (canned)
- bean sprouts
- broccoli (pieces)
- cabbage (shredded)
- carrots or celery (sliced)
- cauliflower (pieces)
- baby corn (canned)
- mushrooms (sliced)
- green onions (chopped)
- frozen peas or whole fresh snow peas
- green pepper (strips)

This meal includes beef broth and soda crackers. You can order this first when you are eating at a Chinese restaurant.

Fill up on the low-calorie vegetable dishes. You may add a bit of soy sauce to your rice if you wish. Fried rice is high in fat. In a restaurant just mix in a bit of fried rice, if you wish.

Stay away from deep-fried, battered foods and foods in sweet sauces.

For dessert, a fortune cookie is a good low-calorie choice. Good luck!

Your Dinner Menu	**Large Meal**	**Small Meal**
Beef broth	1 cup	1 cup
Chinese Stir Fry	2 cups	1 1/2 cups
White rice	1 1/4 cups	3/4 cup
Skim or 1 percent milk	1 cup	1 cup
Pear	1	1
Fortune cookies	2	2

SOLUTIONS WILL COME TO YOU
WHILE YOU ARE WALKING.
SMALL MEAL

DINNER 28

Denver Sandwich & Soup

A sandwich and soup is a light choice for dinner in a restaurant. The sandwich could be a Denver, a club house or a bacon, lettuce and tomato sandwich. Ask for your bread or toast without butter or mayonnaise, or ask the waiter to "go light" on the butter or mayonnaise. Also ask the waiter to hold the french fries. If you want to make a Denver sandwich at home, here's the recipe.

Denver Sandwich

Makes one sandwich.

1 slice (1 ounce) bacon or ham

2 eggs

1 tablespoon chopped parsley, green onion tops, onion or chives

Pepper to taste

2 slices toast, each spread with 1/2 teaspoon butter, margarine or mayonnaise (1 teaspoon if light)

Lettuce

1. Chop the bacon and cook. Drain all fat and soak up extra fat with a paper towel. If you are using chopped ham instead of bacon, you don't need to cook it first.
2. In a small bowl, beat the eggs with a fork. Add the bacon or ham and the parsley or onion tops.
3. Cook in a non-stick pan free of fat. Stir on and off.
4. Place egg mix on piece of toast.
5. Add lettuce or other vegetables to the sandwich.

If you don't care for tomato soup, order vegetable soup or a glass of tomato juice instead. Mushroom and green pea soup have the most calories of all the cream soups. Choose these less often.

These cracker servings have about the same calories:

- 1 bread stick
- 2 soda crackers
- 1 snackbread cracker
- 2 melba toast
- 1 Ritz-like party cracker

There is no dessert with this meal. If you would like to have a small fruit, then omit the bread sticks. Or choose a very low-calorie dessert such as light gelatin or a bought sugar-free popsicle.

Your Dinner Menu	Large Meal	Small Meal
Tomato soup (made with water)	1 cup	1 cup
Bread sticks	1 1/2	1 1/2
Denver Sandwich	1 1/2 sandwiches	1 sandwich
Salad	large	large
Oil-free salad dressing	1 tablespoon	1 tablespoon

SMALL MEAL

DINNER 29

Shish Kebobs

A true Greek shish kebob is called souvlaki and is made only with meat. It would usually be soaked in olive oil, so would be high in calories.

Shish kebobs can be one of the lowest fat meal choices in a Greek or Middle Eastern restaurant. Try this oil-free recipe at home.

Shish Kebob Marinade

Makes enough for two shish kebobs.

2 tablespoons low-fat Italian salad dressing

1 tablespoon lemon juice

2 cloves garlic, crushed or chopped finely (or 1/2 teaspoon garlic powder)

1/4 teaspoon pepper

1/2 teaspoon oregano

1 teaspoon sugar

This recipe could also be made with chunks of lamb or goat (as often used on shish kebobs in Greece), or chicken or fish.

Mix the marinade ingredients together in a dish.

Shish Kebobs

To make each shish kebob you will need:
Meat (1 1/2-inch cubes of lean beef)
For large meal: 4 cubes (6 ounces, raw)
For small meal: 3 cubes (4 ounces, raw)
Vegetables
Cherry tomatoes, whole fresh mushrooms, cubes of green pepper, whole small onions (or chunks of onion), zucchini, eggplant, or any other vegetables you like.

Vegetables added to these shish kebobs help keep the calories lower because you're not filling up on meat.

1. Place the meat in the marinade and let it sit in the fridge for a couple of hours.
2. Put the meat and vegetables on skewers, as shown in the picture. Brush with the marinade. If you want your meat well done, broil or barbecue it for five minutes before adding the vegetables.
3. Broil or barbecue for five to ten minutes or until cooked.

For a change, you can add 1 tablespoon of tomato sauce (see page 190) to your cooked rice.

This Greek Salad includes tomatoes, onions, green pepper, feta cheese and black olives. Feel free to add lettuce also. Traditional Greek salad also has lots of olive oil. This recipe is an oil-free variety.

Greek Salad

Makes two large salads.

If you are having this meal in a restaurant, remember to ask for light salad dressing on the side.

2 large tomatoes, cut in wedges

1/2 medium onion, sliced

1/2 green pepper, in chunks

1/2 small cucumber

1/4 cup feta cheese, crumbled or chunks

4 black olives

2 tablespoons oil-free Italian dressing

Sprinkle of oregano

1. Mix together the tomatoes, onions, green pepper, cucumber, feta cheese and olives.
2. Before serving, add salad dressing and sprinkle with oregano.

This meal ends with a low-fat dessert:
Apple sprinkled with a touch of cinnamon and icing sugar. Instead of apple, you could have an orange or 1/2 cup of cantaloupe, melon or grapes.

Your Dinner Menu	Large Meal	Small Meal
Shish Kebob	1 made with 4 cubes of beef	1 made with 3 cubes of beef
Rice	3/4 cup	3/4 cup
Greek Salad with dressing	1 large	1 large
Crusty white bun	1	–
Margarine	1 teaspoon	–
Cinnamon apple rings	1/2 3-inch apple with 1/2 teaspoon icing sugar plus cinnamon	1/2 3-inch apple with 1/2 teaspoon icing sugar plus cinnamon

SMALL MEAL

DINNER 30

Roti with Curried Filling

***R**otis and chapatis are flat East Indian breads made from flour and water. Two chapatis would equal 1 roti shell. Rotis or chapatis can be bought ready-made from an East Indian or Caribbean restaurant or store.*

***I**f you can't find rotis or chapatis, you can put the filling in 2 pita shells or 2 flour tortillas. 1 1/2 cups of rice could also replace a roti shell.*

***I**n the Caribbean, rotis are served folded around a filling of curried meat, chicken or beans and potatoes. Sometimes the rotis are eaten on the side with a curried dish.*

Here are two ways to serve your cucumbers:
Slice them thinly and put in a bowl with either:
1. *plain skim milk yogurt, flavored with mint or a sprinkle of paprika,*
2. *vinegar, lemon juice or lime juice*

Curried Chick Peas and Potato Filling

Makes 3 cups (enough for six rotis).

1/4 cup water
1 teaspoon vegetable oil
1 medium onion, chopped
2 garlic cloves, finely chopped or crushed
1 tablespoon curry powder (mild or hot)
Dash of hot sauce or chili powder
2 small potatoes, cooked and chopped in small chunks
19 ounce (540 ml) can chick peas, including juice

1. Heat the water and oil in a heavy pot and add the onions, garlic, curry powder and hot sauce. Cook at low heat until the onions are soft.
2. Add the cooked potatoes and canned chickpeas with juice and cook for half an hour. Cool and put in the fridge overnight.

Making the Rotis
The next day, re-heat the Filling and place 1/2 cup in the middle of each roti. Fold one side over the mixture, then the other. Fold ends toward the center to make a neat package. Turn it over on the plate so the folds are underneath. Microwave on high for three to four minutes, or heat in a hot oven for half an hour.

This meal is served with carrot sticks and cucumbers. The large meal also has plantains. Plantains look like large green bananas (see photograph). But unlike a banana, plantains need to be cooked before eating. Plantain is ready to use when it has turned partly black on the outside. Then you can cut it in strips and boil it until soft. Next, lightly brush it with margarine and roast or broil it in the oven. It can also be boiled, then fried in a non-stick pan. It is served as a starchy vegetable (like corn or potatoes).

The dessert for this meal is coconut meringues, which are made with sugar, but no fat—so the calories of this dessert are low. Two of these meringues have about the same amount of sugar and calories as a small piece of fruit.

Coconut Meringues

Makes twenty-eight 2-inch meringues.

1 cup sugar

1/4 tsp cream of tartar

4 egg whites, at room temperature (throw out the yolks)

1/2 teaspoon coconut flavoring

1 tablespoon unsweetened coconut (optional)

1. In a small bowl, mix the sugar with the cream of tartar.
2. Beat the egg whites until stiff. Add the sugar and cream of tartar mixture slowly and continue beating until the mixture forms stiff peaks. Beat in the coconut flavoring.
3. Drop heaping tablespoonfuls onto two ungreased cookie sheets. Sprinkle the coconut on top of the meringues. Bake at 200°F for two hours. After 1 1/2 hours, check to see if they are ready. They should be dry when you poke them with a skewer or toothpick. When they're ready, turn the oven off and let them sit in the oven for another two hours.
4. Once cooled, store in a cookie jar or plastic container.

Your Dinner Menu	Large Meal	Small Meal
Bean & Potato Roti	1 roti	1 roti
Roasted plantain (brushed lightly with 1/2 teaspoon of margarine)	1/2	–
Carrot sticks	1 medium carrot	1/3 medium carrot
Cucumbers (in yogurt)	1/2 medium cucumber plus 2 tablespoons of yogurt	1/2 medium cucumber
Coconut Meringues	2	1

SMALL MEAL

DINNER 31

Tandoori Chicken & Rice

This recipe is also delicious when made with curry powder instead of the tandoori mix. If you use curry powder, the sauce will be a golden curry color. The tandoori mix will make the sauce reddish.

Tandoori chicken can be served with either:

- *rice, as shown in the photograph (Basmati rice, available in most large food stores, is my favorite)*
- *naan, a risen bread that can be bought fresh in some large food stores or restaurants*
- *chapati, an East Indian flat bread similar to roti*

It is important to boil the sauce for five minutes. Raw chicken may carry a lot of bacteria, and boiling will make the sauce safe to eat.

I fell in love with tandoori chicken when I lived in Kenya. This delicious meal is spicy but not hot. The chicken is coated in a tasty low-fat coating and then baked or barbecued. The tandoori chicken is eaten with rice.

Tandoori Chicken and Sauce

Makes 5 large or 8 small servings.

Sauce:

1 1/2 cups plain (white) skim milk yogurt

1 1/2 tablespoons store-bought tandoori spice mix

1 1/2 tablespoons vinegar

1 1/2 tablespoons lemon juice

2 1/2 lbs (1 kg) of chicken, cut in pieces with the skin taken off.

1. In a large bowl or pot, mix all the ingredients for the sauce.
2. Make some small cuts in each chicken piece so the yogurt sauce can flavor the meat. Add the chicken to the bowl or pot, making sure that it is covered with sauce. Cover and place in the fridge for at least four hours, or overnight.
3. Gently shake any extra sauce from the chicken and barbecue or place on a rack in a pan and grill in the oven (about 5 inches from the grill). Cook for ten to fifteen minutes on each side until well done.
4. Put the leftover sauce in a small heavy pan and boil for 5 minutes. Give each person a small dish of this sauce for dunking their chicken and putting on their rice.

A nice finish to this meal is a small piece of tropical fruit, such as mango or papaya.

Serve this meal with herbal or regular tea, or try making this Indian Spiced Tea.

Indian Spiced Tea

Makes 5 cups.

2 tea bags

6 cardamom pods

1 3-inch stick cinnamon

1 teaspoon lemon juice

5 cups boiling water (one teapot full)

1/2 cup hot milk for each serving

1. Place tea, cardamom, cinnamon and lemon juice in your teapot. Fill the pot with boiling water and let steep for four minutes. Remove the bags, the cardamom and the cinnamon from the pot.
2. Serve the tea with an equal part of hot skim milk, and if you want, 1 teaspoon of sugar, honey or low-calorie sweetener.

Poppadums:
If you've never had poppadums, you don't know what you're missing! They can be bought in large food stores and in specialty food stores. They are 5-7 inches round and come in mild or hot (spicy). All you need to do is place them under a hot broiler and in one or two minutes they will bubble and turn a golden brown. Broil both sides. Or run them quickly under tap water to wet them and then pop them in the microwave at high power for about forty seconds. These crunchy treats are great with a curry meal or can be eaten as a snack.

Your Dinner Menu	Large Meal	Small Meal
Tandoori Chicken	1 large leg	1 small leg
Tandoori Sauce	4 tablespoons	2 tablespoons
Rice (Basmati)	1 cup	3/4 cup
Bed of lettuce with tomato and cucumber	1/2 medium tomato and sliced cucumber	1/2 medium tomato and sliced cucumber
Poppadums	2	2
Mango	1/2	1/2
Indian Spiced Tea	1 cup	1 cup

SMALL MEAL

Snacks

Snacks

In this section you will find photographs of four groups of snacks. The groups are low-calorie snacks, small snacks, medium snacks and large snacks. The calories for each snack within each group are about the same. The number of snacks you choose will depend on how many calories a day you want. Look at the chart on page 49 that shows the calories of the small and large meals, and different snacks.

For most of us it's good to choose no more than three of the small, medium or large snacks a day.

Three small snacks add up to 150 calories, three medium snacks add up to 300 calories and three large snacks add up to 600 calories.

Low-calorie snacks:

- These snacks have just 20 calories or less.
  These foods are not fattening. A few of these a day will have little effect on your weight. You may add them to your meals or snacks.

Small snacks:

- These snacks have 50 calories.

Remember:

- *1 medium snack = 2 small snacks*
- *1 large snack = 2 medium snacks, or 4 small snacks*

Medium snacks:

- These snacks have 100 calories.
- Two small snacks would equal one medium snack.

Large snacks:

- These snacks have 200 calories.
- Two medium snacks, or four small snacks, would equal one large snack.

Remember to drink water when you have a snack. And try to avoid late night snacking.

Choose a variety of snacks and you won't get bored. When you eat a snack between meals you will not feel so hungry at meal times. Most of the snacks are low in fat and sugar, just like the meals. A snack made from a milk food will give you important calcium, a bran muffin will give you fibre, and a fruit is full of vitamins.

What about eating candy, chocolates and chips and other foods that are made with lots of fat or sugar? It is okay to have a small amount of these once in a while. But these shouldn't be eaten every day, as they give you calories but little nutrition. On the photographs on pages 224-229 you will find these kinds of foods marked as occasional snacks. Alcoholic drinks are also marked as an occasional snack choice. Remember drinking alcohol does not mix well with some pills (see page 35).

If you have diabetes and you take insulin or a diabetes pill in the evening, read this: An evening snack that has some protein or fat will help prevent low blood sugar in the middle of the night. Ask your doctor or dietitian for more advice.

In the photograph of each snack group are snacks with about the same number of calories. But some of the snacks have different amounts of sugar or starch, protein or fat.

In the small, medium and large photographs, you will find:

- starchy snacks which have mostly starch
- fruit and vegetable snacks which have natural sugar
- milk snacks have natural milk sugar and protein; and some may have some fat
- mixed snacks which are a mix of foods from different food groups, such as a starch and a protein
- occasional snacks that are high in fat or sugar, or that have alcohol.

Low-calorie snacks

20 calories or less in each snack

Drinks

1. water is your best low-calorie snack
2. diet soft drinks and packaged diet drink mixes
3. herbal tea
4. coffee or tea (regular or decaffeinated)—have your coffee or tea black or add a small amount of low-fat milk, skim milk powder or light whitener. Cut back on sugar and try a low-calorie sweetener instead.
5. bouillon or broth—you may want to look for low-salt brands.

Additions to your meals or snacks

6. low-calorie sweeteners
7. flavorings, such as cocoa, spices and herbs
8. 1 teaspoon mustard, relish or ketchup
9. hot sauce
10. vinegar
11. 1 tablespoon salsa
12. 1 teaspoon honey, jam, jelly or syrup (diet jam or diet syrup will have less sugar)
13. 1 tablespoon bran—added to cereal, soups and stews and cereals; this will give you extra fiber
14. 1 tablespoon whipped or frozen topping (or 1 tablespoon of light sour cream or 2 tablespoon of fat-free sour cream)
15. 1 tablespoon oil-free salad dressing

Other Snacks

16. 1/4 sauerkraut
17. 1 cup salad greens
18. 1 soda cracker
19. 1/2 cup Jellied Vegetable Salad (see recipe page 139)
20. half a tomato
21. 1/2 cup light gelatin
22. 1 piece sugar-free or regular gum
23. 1 mint or small hard candy
24. several mini-mints
25. 1 sugar-free popsicle
26. 2 green olives
27. 3 radishes
28. 1 dill pickle
29. lemon and lime
30. a stalk of celery
31. 1/2 cucumber

Small snacks

50 calories in each snack

Vegetables

Always have raw, washed vegetables in the fridge. The vegetables should be ready-to-eat and easy to grab.

1. 3/4 cup Coleslaw (page 80)
2. 1 stalk celery with 1 tablespoon cheese spread
3. large salad with 1 tablespoon fat-free salad dressing
4. 1 medium carrot
5. 1 cup canned tomatoes

Fruit

6. 1 cup of strawberries
7. 1 small orange
8. 1/2 large grapefruit
9. 1/2 medium apple
10. 1 medium plum
11. 1 medium kiwi
12. 2 prunes (or figs)
13. 2 tablespoons raisins
14. 2-inch piece of banana
15. 3/4 cup Light Gelatin with Fruit (page 183)
16. 3/4 cup Stewed Rhubarb (page 107)

Juice

17. 1 cup tomato or vegetable juice
18. 1/2 cup unsweetened fruit juice (try mixing the juice with some sparkling water or diet ginger ale)

Milk snacks

19. 1/2 cup low-fat fruit yogurt sweetened with a low-calorie sweetener
20. 1 cup light hot cocoa
21. 1/2 cup low-fat milk (skim or 1 percent)
22. 1 light fudge ice cream bar, revello or creamsicle (made with a low-calorie sweetener)

Starchy snacks

23. 1 cup puffed wheat cereal
24. 1 cup of packaged soup
25. 2 bread sticks
26. 1 rice cake
27. 1 digestive cookie or other plain cookie
28. 2 medium crackers
29. 2 melba toast
30. 4 soda crackers
31. 1 fibre crispbread
32. 2 Graham wafer halves
33. 2 poppadums

Occasional snacks

34. 1 chocolate chip cookie
35. 1 fig bar
36. 1/4 cup (21) fish crackers
37. 3 hard candy mints
38. 5 lifesavers
39. a small chocolate
40. 2 marshmallows
41. 3 ounces dry table wine

Medium snacks

100 calories in each snack
(two small snacks from the last photograph will equal one medium snack)

Vegetables:

1. 2-3 cups of raw vegetables with 2 tablespoons of Vegetable Dip (page 171)

Fruits

2. 1/2 medium cantaloupe
3. 1 cup applesauce
4. 4 pineapple rings plus 2 tablespoon juice
5. 1 small banana
6. 3 figs
7. 5 dried apricots
8. 1 pear
9. 1 cup fresh fruit salad
10. 4 thin slices watermelon
11. 1 1/2 cup grapes

Starchy foods

12. 1 slice raisin toast with 1 teaspoon of margarine
13. 3 arrowroots or other plain cookies
14. 6 pretzels
15. 1 waffle or crumpet with 1 teaspoon jam
16. 3 cups air-popped popcorn
17. 1 whole wheat roll with cucumber, tomato, lettuce
18. 1/3 of an 80 gram package of oriental noodles
19. 1 slice matzo bread
20. 8 baked tortilla chips or other baked chips with 1 tablespoon salsa sauce

Mixed snacks

21. Half of a pizza bun
22. 1 piece toast with 1 teaspoon peanut butter
23. 1/2 cup 1 percent cottage cheese and 1/2 tomato
24. 1 cup canned tomatoes and 2 tablespoons shredded cheese
25. 2/3 cup oat o's cereal and 1/2 cup low-fat milk

26. 1/2 cup low-fat milk and 2 gingersnaps
27. 8 jumbo shrimp and 2 tablespoons of shrimp cocktail sauce
28. 4 soda crackers and 1/2 ounce Edam cheese
29. 2 wheat crackers with 1 tablespoon light cream cheese

Milk snacks

30. 1 cup low-fat milk (including buttermilk)
31. 3/4 cup light pudding (also nice frozen in a popsicle stick)
32. 3/4 cup low-fat yogurt

Occasional snacks

33. 1 serving Chocolate Mousse (page 119) and 1/2 ice wafer
34. 3 by 2-inch piece of rice crispie marshmallow square
35. low-fat granola bar
36. 1 light beer (12 oz or 355 ml)
37. 1 1/2 ounce rye, gin, rum, whiskey or other alcohol (mixed with diet pop or water)
38. 1 piece angel food cake
39. 2 1/2 licorice sticks
40. 10 jelly beans
41. 3 chocolate pieces (20 grams in total)

Large Snacks

200 calories in each snack
(two medium snacks from the last photograph will equal one large snack)

Mixed snacks

1. Vegetable and cracker bowl: 2 cups any kind of raw vegetables with 3 snackbreads, 2 bread sticks and 3 tablespoons Vegetable Dip (page 171).
2. 2 slices toast with 1 teaspoon of butter or margarine and 2 teaspoons of jam
3. 1 cup cream of wheat hot cereal and 3/4 cup low-fat milk
4. 1 piece Crustless Pumpkin Pie (page 159) with 2 tablespoons whipped topping
5. 1 small cone with 3/4 cup light ice cream
6. 1 Bran Muffin (page 64) and 1/2 ounce cheese
7. 1 piece Bannock (page 115) and 1 teaspoon jam
8. 16 fresh peanuts
9. 1 slice pumpernickel bread with 1 teaspoon of margarine and 1 1/2 ounces pickled herring
10. 1 cup low-fat milk or buttermilk plus 3 plain cookies
11. 1 cup Rice Pudding (page 111)
12. large cob of corn with 1 teaspoon of butter or margarine
13. small baked potato with 1 tablespoon light sour cream
14. 1 Baked Apple (page 147) plus 1/2 ounce cheese
15. 4 crackers with 2 large sardines
16. 1/2 can cream of tomato soup made with low-fat milk, and 2 soda crackers
17. 1 ounce cheese and asparagus on bread
18. 1 shredded wheat with 1/2 small banana and 1/2 cup low-fat milk
19. 1/2 bagel with 2 tablespoons of light cream cheese

20. mixed nuts as shown
21. 16 baked tortilla chips and 2 tablespoons of hummus or salsa
22. ham sandwich (1 ounce meat, no margarine) with mustard and lettuce
23. 1 egg and 1 toast with 1 teaspoon margarine (1 teaspoon jam is optional)
24. 1 ounce cheese and fruit pieces

Fruits

25. Two fruits, such as a small apple and a pear.

Occasional snacks

26. small cake donut
27. cheesies (about 25)
28. potato chips (about 18)
29. 40g chocolate bar

Index

Meals for Good Health Manual

If you would like more detailed information about the nutritional advice in *Meals for Good Health* you may want to order the *Meals for Good Health Manual*. This guide book is useful if you are a health care worker or educator, or if you are a consumer wanting more nutrition information. This booklet includes the following:

- calorie and nutrient listings of meals, snacks and recipes; key meal nutrients are highlighted
- Canadian Diabetes Association Food Choice Values for all meals, recipes and snacks
- list of other useful nutrition resources
- how to adapt the meals in *Meals for Good Health* for children, teenagers, and pregnant women
- background to the development of *Meals for Good Health* (needs, goals, objectives and community evaluation)

COST: $19.95 *(plus $6.75 GST and shipping and handling)*
To order, send a cheque or money order to:

Paper Birch Publishing
89 Wilkinson Crescent
Portage la Prairie, Manitoba R1N 1A7

You can also order the *Meals for Good Health Manual* from your local Canadian Diabetes Association or call **toll-free: 1-800-BANTING** (1-800-226-8464)

For more information visit this website:
http://www.nald.ca